NFTs for Business

A Practical Guide to Harnessing Digital Assets

Ahmed Bouzid
Paolo Narciso
Steve Wood

NFTs for Business: A Practical Guide to Harnessing Digital Assets

Ahmed Bouzid
McLean, VA, USA

Paolo Narciso
Seabrook Island, SC, USA

Steve Wood
Cincinnati, OH, USA

ISBN-13 (pbk): 978-1-4842-9776-6
https://doi.org/10.1007/978-1-4842-9777-3

ISBN-13 (electronic): 978-1-4842-9777-3

Managing Director, Apress Media LLC: Welmoed Spahr
Acquisitions Editor: Shiva Ramachandran
Development Editor: James Markham
Editorial Project Manager: Shaul Elson

Cover designed by eStudioCalamar

Distributed to the book trade worldwide by Springer Science+Business Media New York, 1 New York Plaza, Suite 4600, New York, NY 10004-1562, USA. Phone 1-800-SPRINGER, fax (201) 348-4505, e-mail orders-ny@springer-sbm.com, or visit www.springeronline.com. Apress Media, LLC is a California LLC and the sole member (owner) is Springer Science + Business Media Finance Inc (SSBM Finance Inc). SSBM Finance Inc is a **Delaware** corporation.

For information on translations, please e-mail booktranslations@springernature.com; for reprint, paperback, or audio rights, please e-mail bookpermissions@springernature.com.

Apress titles may be purchased in bulk for academic, corporate, or promotional use. eBook versions and licenses are also available for most titles. For more information, reference our Print and eBook Bulk Sales web page at http://www.apress.com/bulk-sales.

Any source code or other supplementary material referenced by the author in this book is available to readers on GitHub. For more detailed information, please visit https://www.apress.com/gp/services/source-code.

Paper in this product is recyclable

To our families, friends, and fellow Web3 travelers

Table of Contents

About the Authors

Dr. Ahmed Bouzid has been closely following the NFT world for the last two years and has written on the topic and has interviewed several professionals in the space for his podcast. He is also launching the very first pure audio-based NFT marketplace through Witlingo, his digital audio and voicebot products and solutions startup. The main users that Witlingo's NFT marketplace is targeting are podcasters, voice actors and artists, singers, comedians, and other professionals who make their living using voice and audio.

Dr. Paolo Narciso has been building solutions using NFTs for nearly four years. His work involves developing a technology credentialing system that allows students to "earn while they learn." In addition to developing solutions, he created a hybrid community and online program to teach underserved talent how to develop for Web3 with the mission of educating the next generation of diverse architects, builders, and creators for the coming tech revolution.

Steve Wood has been following the progress of NFTs since 2018. He helped create an NFT rating protocol, a game rewards system that uses NFTs to provide digital "gold medals," and was part of the development of Liberland's governance system which leverages NFTs for several functions. He has launched multiple tokens and an L1 blockchain and has deployed a token protocol built to facilitate providing real liquid value to NFTs.

Acknowledgments

My thanks go first to my two co-authors and to our editors for making this project a pleasure to work on. I am especially thankful to Shivangi Ramachandran, who initially engaged with us and helped us pitch the book to her team, and to Sowmya Thodur, who expertly and patiently guided us through the process.

Among the many generous Web3 experts who engaged with me and taught me many things, I would like to especially thank the following: Bertrand Portier, Brady Gentile, David Shuttleworth, Drew Riester, Jimmy Dendrinos, Kiefer Zang, Olivia Baker, Pamela Norton, Randy Sosin, Rob McCarty, Shannon Wu, Sumya Ojakli, Wendy Overton, and Zenobia Godschalk.

Among my friends who provided advice, inspiration, and moral support, I thank Ahmed Ahmed-Yahia, Chawki Belkhodja, David Ferro, Eskinder W. Sahle, Yonael D. Teklu, Harold Young-On, Jay Yeo, Karkar Badreddine, Karim Seferdjeli, Nadira Boumechal, Rachid Darradji, Rajiv Bammi, Samuel K. Kassegne, and Steve Fuller.

Last and most, to my parents and my siblings – Kamel, Reda, and Souad.

—Ahmed Bouzid

ACKNOWLEDGMENTS

Writing a book is seldom a solo journey, and this work on NFTs is no exception. I am indebted to many for their invaluable contributions, guidance, and inspiration.

First and foremost, I would like to express my profound gratitude to my co-authors, Dr. Ahmed Bouzid and Steve Wood. Working alongside these brilliant minds, I have learned immensely and grown as an author and a researcher. Their insights, patience, and encouragement shaped this book in more ways than one can quantify.

My explorations into the world of NFTs were heavily influenced by the insightful work of Chris Dixon, the founder of a16z. His pioneering spirit and visionary approach have consistently shed light on the intricacies of the evolving digital landscape. Additionally, I was inspired by the countless crypto startups that are sculpting the face of the future. Notably, my son-in-law's venture, Triangle Labs, which offers a fresh perspective on Web3 possibilities, has been a beacon of innovation.

Another source of immense inspiration was Shermin Voshmgir's book, *Token Economy*. In my perspective, it stands as one of the finest texts on Web3, breaking down the complexities of the digital realm with eloquence and clarity.

Away from the world of crypto and NFTs, I owe a depth of gratitude to my family and friends. Their unwavering support, occasional distractions, and ceaseless encouragement were the bedrock upon which I rested during the most challenging moments of this journey. Special thanks to Dr. Rev. Paul Siaki, whose guidance has always grounded me, and the trumpet maestro Leonard Montgomery, whose melodies and musings on the app Marco Polo both distracted and inspired me, serving as a musical backdrop to many a writing session.

To everyone mentioned and the countless others who touched this journey in ways big and small: thank you, this book is as much yours as it is mine.

—Paolo Narciso

I would like to thank my co-authors Drs. Ahmed Bouzid and Paolo Narciso for their support in bringing this book to life. This is my first book written with multiple authors. Their reviews of my contributions, help in connecting with experts to provide additional insights, writing of large portions of the manuscript, and more all made this possible.

Furthermore, everyone who has contributed to the depth of my knowledge regarding blockchain generally and NFTs specifically deserves a shout-out. My good friend and business partner Jean-Philippe Beaudet has been the single largest contributor to my understanding of Web3 technologies from a technical point of view. Special thanks are also due to David Shuttleworth, Managing Director of Binance Labs, for his perspective and insights on the future direction of NFTs.

Additional credit is due to my colleagues Abraham Choi, Michal Ptáčník, and others who worked with me in detail over several years, which helped me understand the vast breadth of practical use cases blockchain technology and NFTs can offer. Without all these individuals, my contributions to this book would not have been possible.

Of course, no acknowledgment would be complete without due credit to my wife Ammy – thank you for wrangling our children while I worked on this manuscript over many long days and weekends.

—Steve Wood

Introduction

The Decentralized Dawn

Every once in a while, a revolutionary technology emerges, transforming the way we perceive, interact, and engage with the world. Not long ago, the Internet – Web 1.0 – shifted our reality, introducing an era of information, replacing print media with online content. Then came the advent of Web 2.0, or the "social web," which ushered in the age of interactivity, user-generated content, and social networking. As powerful as these shifts were, we are now standing on the precipice of an even more seismic change, one that promises to redefine our digital existence – the advent of Web 3.0.

Web 3.0, also known as the "semantic Web" or the "decentralized Internet," aims to create an ownership layer to the Internet, adding qualities of uniqueness, conciseness, privacy, and value which were difficult to create in previous iterations of the Web but are so crucial to the human experience in the physical world. It also seeks to democratize the Web, moving it from a centralized paradigm that is increasingly governed by tech giants and intermediaries to a decentralized one where users regain control over their own digital lives.

This narrative is incomplete without the mention of blockchain technology, the key enabler of this decentralization. Initially popularized as the underlying architecture for Bitcoin, blockchain's potential stretches far beyond digital currencies. It is the foundation for a completely decentralized digital economy, underpinning everything from online payments to decentralized apps (dApps), decentralized autonomous organizations (DAOs), and non-fungible tokens (NFTs).

Today, we can see hints of what Web 3.0 will offer. Online payments like PayPal or credit card transactions are becoming instant and secure, offering a taste of digital transactions' speed and efficiency. Generative AI and chatbots exemplify the semantic Web's onset, where inquiries receive precise responses rather than exhaustive documents. Secure communication apps like Signal and Telegram underscore the increasing need for privacy and data control. We've also started paying directly for the value we consume, be it news articles behind paywalls or streaming services like Netflix, moving away from the ad-based revenue model.

These examples, as promising as they may be, barely scratch the surface of what Web 3.0 aspires to achieve. Their implementation still leans on the Web 2.0 stack, struggling with limitations like servers, power consumption, and centralized control. Nevertheless, they offer a glimpse of Web 3.0's promise – a decentralized, scalable, and sustainable digital landscape where individuals and organizations prosper by taking control of their digital assets and attributes.

The most mainstream manifestation of Web 3.0 to date is cryptocurrency. Even its most ardent critics are starting to acknowledge its presence, and tech giants, far from resisting, are embracing the potential of a more decentralized tech ecosystem. Cryptocurrency solves some problems far more effectively than others, signifying why its adoption isn't evenly distributed. Yet, despite the challenges, the technology's promise is too compelling to ignore.

That promise is embodied in programs and applications, commonly known as "smart contracts," living and running on blockchains. Navigating this complex domain of smart contracts is David Shuttleworth, a veteran in the field and current Managing Director at Binance Labs. His experience with behavioral economics research and across Consensys' product suite lends a unique perspective to our understanding of these digital protocols. However, NFTs are the implementation of smart contracts where Shuttleworth finds real excitement.

Shuttleworth's excitement stems from the story of NFTs' evolution, beginning as static assets and becoming the utility-enabled entities they are today. He believes the introduction of the ERC-6551 standard in May 2023 marked a leap forward in NFT functionality. "Now you can have an NFT that owns other assets," he emphasizes.

This has ushered in a realm of extended functionality for NFTs, from signing multisignature transactions to registering Ethereum Name Services (ENS) domains, or even participating in voting. Shuttleworth sees ERC-6551 as a game-changer in onboarding non-Web3 native people, "Now, [brands] have a way to onboard people by taking away a step where you have to create a MetaMask wallet or a Trust wallet. The NFT can do the heavy lifting."

Composability is a key feature of ERC-6551. "With the new functionality of ERC-6551, brands can say they want to partner with a protocol and give their customers an NFT that is immediately composable with other social spaces," Shuttleworth highlights. This opens doors for any entity to issue NFTs with immediate utility and value, such as allowing holders to participate in governance. But he reminds us that meaningful engagement is essential, "If you don't have something interesting to vote on, people aren't going to participate."

However, we must recognize that blockchain technologies, including cryptocurrencies, smart contracts, dApps, DAOs, and NFTs, are in a state of imperfection; they have flaws and occasionally appear to behave irrationally. Yet, it's undeniable that something substantial is taking shape – a transformation that is as wonderful as it is potentially disruptive.

One such area of transformation lies in the realm of art and collectibles. NFTs have shown their profound impact, enabling artists to tokenize their digital creations and sell them directly to patrons. NFTs not only monetize art but also give artists greater control over their intellectual property, promising a future where art's value is dictated by the creator and their audience rather than traditional intermediaries.

This paradigm shift isn't limited to art. The music industry is witnessing the benefits of NFTs, with musicians tokenizing their songs and albums and issuing limited editions of their works. These NFTs often include bonus tracks and behind-the-scenes content, creating a unique experience for the listener.

Gaming and virtual worlds have also embraced NFTs. The tokenization of in-game assets has become increasingly popular, enabling verifiable ownership and the transfer of items across multiple gaming platforms. In conjunction with virtual and augmented reality, blockchain technology is set to create immersive gaming experiences with NFTs playing a critical role.

NFTs are also driving innovation in ownership models. Fractional ownership allows multiple individuals to own a piece of a high-value digital asset, democratizing access to rare collectibles and virtual real estate. Furthermore, NFTs can enhance liquidity by enabling seamless trading and instant transfers.

Another exciting frontier is digital identity and personal branding. NFTs, in combination with social tokens, can serve as verifiable proof of ownership, expertise, and accomplishments. By offering unique benefits to their supporters, individuals can strengthen their personal brand and cultivate a loyal following.

However, the journey toward a decentralized Web 3.0 is riddled with challenges. From a lack of awareness and technical complexity to market volatility and environmental concerns, the path is far from smooth. Moreover, trust and verification issues, coupled with intellectual property challenges, add another layer of complexity.

It's clear that the pace of NFT adoption will depend on how quickly we can navigate these hurdles. Education plays a critical role in breaking down misconceptions and instilling a deeper understanding of NFTs and their benefits. Similarly, building trust through standardized verification processes and blockchain-based provenance records is vital for NFT credibility.

Market stability is another significant concern. Inflated prices due to speculative investors and a general lack of understanding about NFTs have created a volatile market environment. Establishing responsible investment practices and mechanisms to determine the true value of NFTs is crucial for sustainable growth.

Technical complexities pose their challenges too. The process of creating, buying, and selling NFTs often involves interactions with cryptocurrency wallets, decentralized exchanges, and blockchain networks, deterring nontechnical users. Simplifying the user experience is thus essential for broader adoption.

Scalability and network congestion issues can also hinder NFT adoption. Potential solutions include exploring alternative consensus mechanisms, adopting layer-two solutions, developing more scalable blockchains, and establishing interoperability protocols.

While the challenges are considerable, the promise of Web 3.0 and blockchain technologies is compelling. We are at a pivotal point in our digital evolution, where we have the chance to shape the Internet's future, and more importantly, our digital identities. The decentralization, transparency, and control that Web 3.0 promises could fundamentally alter our interaction with the digital world.

The Book at a Glance

This book aims to guide you through this revolution, unveiling the potential of NFTs while discussing their challenges and exploring possible solutions. As we journey through the nascent realm of Web 3.0, I invite you to keep an open mind and a spirit of curiosity. Together, we can anticipate, understand, and shape the dawn of the decentralized digital era.

The book also delves into blockchain's fascinating intricacies, demystifying complex terms and concepts to make them accessible to the uninitiated reader. The aim is to equip readers with a solid grasp of blockchain's foundational principles and the mechanics that drive its operation. This means, among other things, exploring blockchain's origins and charting its evolution.

At its core, blockchain represents a paradigm shift from centralized to decentralized systems. We will delve into the implications of this shift, exploring how it impacts trust, control, and agency in our digital lives. By demonstrating how blockchain technology brings about decentralization, the reader will gain an understanding of the transformative power of the technology underlying NFTs and why it is fundamental to the next iteration of the Web.

We must also turn our attention to cryptocurrencies. This requires us to navigate the multifaceted world of digital currencies, from Bitcoin to the vast array of altcoins each with their own use cases, challenges, and potential, as well as their role in fostering a decentralized digital economy. The aim is not necessarily to demystify cryptocurrencies, but to place them within the broader context of the environment in which NFTs exist.

Smart contracts and dApps also feature prominently in our exploration. By automating the execution of agreements and facilitating peer-to-peer interactions, these technologies symbolize blockchain's potential to revolutionize various sectors, from finance and law to supply chain and entertainment. We examine the functioning, uses, and impact of these technologies, shedding light on their current and future potential.

Decentralized autonomous organizations (DAOs) represent another intriguing aspect of the decentralized Web. As organizations run by smart contracts, DAOs promise a future where companies can operate transparently and democratically, without centralized control. We delve into the nature of DAOs, their advantages and challenges, and their role in shaping future organizational structures.

After that we turn our focus primarily to the main topic of interest – non-fungible tokens (NFTs) themselves. We embark on a comprehensive exploration of NFTs, delving into their creation, functioning, and use cases. We then traverse diverse domains, from art and music to gaming and virtual reality, investigating how NFTs are revolutionizing these fields.

This exploration of NFTs is not confined only to their present applications. We envisage potential future use cases, contemplating how NFTs could redefine concepts of ownership, value, and interactivity in the digital realm. The exploration of NFTs is comprehensive, offering readers a holistic understanding of their potential and implications while remaining focused primarily on business-level interests over technical considerations.

Moreover, this book delves into the broader social, economic, and political implications of these technologies. As they redefine concepts of value, ownership, and power, these technologies can potentially disrupt existing structures and systems, eliciting a myriad of responses from different stakeholders.

The book certainly intends to cast an eye to the future, speculating on the long-term impact and potential evolution of Web 3.0, blockchain, and NFTs. Through an informed and thoughtful exploration, we aim to provide readers with insights that can help them navigate this rapidly evolving landscape.

Ultimately, this book seeks to provide readers with a comprehensive, balanced, and accessible guide to the revolutionary world of Web 3.0. As we explore this new transformation sweeping through the Internet, we aim to equip readers with the knowledge and understanding they need to embrace this transformation and make the most of its immense potential.

Whether you're a curious observer eager to understand the buzzwords that have invaded our digital discourse or a seasoned technophile intent on grasping the nuances of the latest tech revolution, this book aims to be your compass, guiding you through the labyrinth of the decentralized digital world.

INTRODUCTION

As we stand at the threshold of Web 3.0's growing commercialization, there is much to anticipate, much to understand, and much to shape. The promise of a more democratic, transparent, and inclusive digital world is within reach. It's time to embrace the dawn of the decentralized era.

CHAPTER 1

Problems Solved by NFTs

Non-fungible tokens (NFTs) are digital assets that can come in the form of art, music, in-game items, videos, and more and seem to be everywhere these days. From art and music to tacos and toilet paper, these digital assets are selling like 17th-century exotic Dutch tulips – some for millions of dollars.

So, when you create something new, you should be rewarded for the effort in proportion to the value that you have created. For that to happen, we need to replicate the constraints of the physical world into the digital world. That is, we need to introduce scarcity, identify ownership, validate authenticity, trace back provenance, and enable the collection of royalties, which is the basis of this chapter.

Introduction

It is a truism to state that the rate of technological innovation has been accelerating at an unprecedented pace. A new technology not only solves a given set of problems, but also paves the way for the creation of new tools for the next generation of innovations. The most obvious example is the personal computer. When initially introduced, the PC was a gadget that helped you do the things that you already did, but do them more efficiently: type without having to deal with typewriters that needed paper

A. Bouzid et al., *NFTs for Business*, https://doi.org/10.1007/978-1-4842-9777-3_1

and ink and white-out liquids (and that broke down every once in a while); calculate without needing a calculator; create balance sheets without pencils, pens, paper, and rulers; learn without having to go to the library; or play games without having to go to the arcade.

But very quickly, the PC became a platform that enabled further innovation in its own right. High-level programming languages such as BASIC, FORTRAN, COBOL, and Pascal enabled anyone willing to learn them to write new software that delivered new solutions to existing problems. Such software (for instance, AutoCAD) enabled its users to experiment faster and with minimal cost. This enabled the creation of yet newer solutions, which then themselves became the next generation of innovation engines.

We are now well into the fifth decade since the introduction of that first generation of PCs in the late 1970s. Since then, we have seen several waves of innovation, each opening up new vistas of possibilities, along with the ecosystem of challenges that emerge as a result of the market's adoption of the products and solutions to which some of those possibilities converted: the Internet, the Web, Wi-Fi connectivity, cell phones, the cloud, smartphones, and the mobile apps that they run, and most recently social networks.

But what is new about this fifth decade is the reality that nearly everything that we do, day in and day out, at nearly every waking moment of our day (and even when we sleep, if we include devices that monitor and collect our vital signs during our slumber) involves us engaged in doing something with a digital device – whether a desktop, a laptop, a surface, a smartphone, a smart speaker, or a wearable device. We interact with our fellow human beings, buy our stuff, plan our trips, organize political movements, listen to our music, do our work, order our food, learn, play, and everything else imaginable, almost entirely in the digital world.

And indeed, we have come a long way since the days of Radio Shack's TRS-80, the Commodore PET, and the Atari 800, both in terms of the hardware, the software, and the plumbing that is enabling our world to keep on turning. But what has remained nearly unaddressed in any meaningful way is the misalignment between several core attributes of the digital ecosystem and the fundamental pillars upon which our economic value chain delivery system rests.

Elemental to the digital world is near zero-cost and instant replication: I can replicate a file as many times as I want in no time and at virtually no cost. I can distribute those files in any way I wish. Those who receive those files can do likewise: they can replicate and distribute those files in any way they wish. In all of this, scarcity, ownership, authenticity, provenance, and royalties collection become either meaningless concepts or nearly impossible to establish. Until the time when wealth distribution no longer relies on labor (and no one is holding their breath for such a system to emerge any time soon), humanity must adopt a mechanism to enable the value exchanges on which our economy relies that works for our increasingly digital reality.

Scarcity

Scarcity refers to the concept of limited availability or a shortage of resources in relation to the demand for those resources. In economics, scarcity is a fundamental concept that affects the decisions individuals, businesses, and governments make about how to allocate resources effectively.

In the digital world, scarcity is often a problem, since digital goods can be easily reproduced without limit. This means that once an original digital asset is created, it can be copied infinitely, leading to a lack of scarcity and a corresponding decrease in value.

NFTs provide digital scarcity by creating unique, noninterchangeable digital assets. This means that each NFT is unique and cannot be replicated, which helps to establish its value. NFTs can be used to represent a variety of digital assets, including art, music, video games, and more. For example, an artist can create a unique piece of digital art and sell it as an NFT, ensuring that there is only one authentic copy of that piece of art in existence. Yes, replicas will exist – just as they exist in the physical world – but unlike the physical world, the digital world can solve the problem of determining whether something is an original or a copy of that original.

An example of an NFT that has achieved significant value is the CryptoPunks collection. CryptoPunks are a series of 10,000 unique digital characters that were created on the Ethereum blockchain. Each CryptoPunk is one of a kind, and some of them have sold for millions of dollars.

Another example is the digital artist Beeple, who sold a single NFT artwork for $69 million at a Christie's auction in March 2021. This sale demonstrated the potential value of unique, noninterchangeable digital assets and the ability of NFTs to create scarcity in the digital world.

A third example is the NBA Top Shot, a blockchain-based platform that allows users to buy, sell, and trade NFTs in the form of video highlights of NBA basketball games. Each highlight is a unique NFT, and the scarcity of each highlight is ensured by the limited number of moments available for each game. The popularity of NBA Top Shot has exploded, with some moments selling for hundreds of thousands of dollars.

And one more is Decentraland, a virtual reality platform built on the Ethereum blockchain that allows users to buy, sell, and trade virtual land parcels as NFTs. Each land parcel is unique and cannot be replicated, creating scarcity in the virtual world. Users can use their land parcels to build virtual experiences, such as games, art galleries, and more, and monetize their creations by selling them as NFTs. The value of each land parcel is determined by its location, size, and the content that is built on it.

Ownership

Ownership refers to the legal and ethical right of an individual or entity to claim control and possession of a tangible or intangible asset. Traditionally, ownership has been associated with physical objects such as a house, a car, or a piece of land. In the digital world, however, ownership often refers to the ability to control and claim ownership of digital assets, such as images, videos, music, podcasts, software, and other types of digital content.

The digital world has brought about many challenges in regard to ownership. Unlike physical assets, digital assets can be easily replicated, shared, and distributed. This has made it difficult for individuals and businesses to claim ownership of their digital assets and control how they are used and distributed. The ease of digital reproduction has also led to issues of copyright infringement and intellectual property theft, making it challenging for artists and creators to monetize their work and protect their rights.

NFTs have emerged as a solution to the problem of ownership in the digital world. By creating a one-of-a-kind token for a specific digital asset, NFTs not only allow for the creation of digital scarcity, but also unique ownership of digital assets.

NFTs solve the problem of ownership in the digital world by providing a way to prove ownership and authenticity of digital assets. NFTs provide a way for artists, musicians, and creators to sell and monetize their digital creations as unique, one-of-a-kind assets. NFTs also provide a way for collectors to claim ownership of digital collectibles, such as trading cards, limited-edition collectibles, and rare in-game items.

Here are five examples of how NFTs solve the problem of ownership in the digital world:

Digital Art: NFTs allow artists to prove ownership and authenticity of their digital artwork, providing a way to sell and trade their digital creations as unique, one-of-a-kind assets. For example, the artist Beeple

5

sold a digital artwork called "Everydays: The First 5000 Days" for $69 million as an NFT.

Collectibles: NFTs allow collectors to claim ownership of digital collectibles, such as trading cards, limited-edition items, and rare in-game items. For example, the NBA has created NBA Top Shot, a platform for buying and selling digital collectibles in the form of NFTs.

Music: NFTs provide a way for musicians and music producers to claim ownership of their music, sell unique experiences, and control the distribution of their music. For example, the musician Grimes sold an NFT collection that included unreleased music and art for nearly $6 million.

Virtual real estate: NFTs allow for ownership of virtual real estate in online games and virtual worlds, providing a way for players to own and trade virtual assets. For example, the virtual world Decentraland allows players to buy and sell virtual land as NFTs.

Domain names: NFTs allow for the ownership and transfer of domain names, providing a way for individuals and businesses to claim and sell unique domain names as one-of-a-kind assets. For example, the domain name "eth.com" was sold for $2 million as an NFT.

Authenticity

Authenticity is a concept that has been widely discussed in various fields, including art, literature, and philosophy. At its core, authenticity refers to the quality of being genuine, real, or true to oneself or an original source. In the digital world, authenticity is a critical issue that has emerged due to the ease of creating, copying, and sharing digital content. This has led to a proliferation of fake or counterfeit digital content, making it challenging to distinguish between what is genuine and what is not. In recent years, the emergence of NFTs has revolutionized the way authenticity is perceived and managed in the digital world.

NFTs are digital tokens that are used to represent ownership of a unique or rare asset or piece of content. NFTs are designed to solve the problem of authenticity in the digital world by providing a unique and tamper-proof record of ownership that cannot be duplicated or replicated.

Here are five examples that illustrate how NFTs are solving the problem of authenticity in the digital world:

> Digital art: In the past, digital artists have struggled to prove ownership of their work and receive proper compensation for their creations. With NFTs, digital artists can create unique tokens for each of their pieces of work, providing a secure record of ownership that cannot be duplicated or replicated.

> Music: NFTs are also being used in the music industry to provide a secure record of ownership for rare or exclusive music tracks. NFTs can be used to represent ownership of the original recording, providing an opportunity for artists to monetize their work and control its distribution.

7

Gaming: In the gaming industry, NFTs are being used to represent ownership of in-game items and virtual assets. Players can buy and sell NFTs for rare or exclusive items, providing a secure record of authentic ownership and creating a new market for digital collectibles.

Sports: NFTs are also being used in the sports industry to represent ownership of rare or exclusive memorabilia, such as game-worn jerseys or autographed items. NFTs provide a secure and verifiable record of ownership, allowing fans to buy and sell unique sports memorabilia in a transparent and secure marketplace.

Real estate: NFTs are also being used in the real estate industry to represent ownership of unique or exclusive properties. NFTs can be used to provide a secure and tamper-proof record of ownership, making it easier for buyers and sellers to transfer ownership of high-value properties.

Provenance

Provenance refers to the history of ownership and custody of a particular object or artifact, including its origin, the chain of custody, and any changes that may have occurred over time. In the world of art, for example, provenance is used to establish the authenticity, ownership, and history of a work of art, which is critical in determining its value. In the digital world, provenance refers to the history of ownership and changes made to a digital asset, such as a document, image, or video. It is essential in determining the authenticity, integrity, and ownership of a digital asset, which is becoming increasingly important as digital assets become more valuable and ubiquitous.

The problem of provenance in the digital world arises because digital assets are easy to replicate and manipulate, and it is difficult to establish the originality and ownership of a digital asset. This makes it easy for people to create and distribute fake or altered digital assets, which can be used for fraudulent purposes, such as identity theft, intellectual property theft, and financial fraud. In addition, it is difficult to track the ownership and history of a digital asset, which can lead to disputes over ownership and control.

NFTs have emerged as a solution to the problem of provenance in the digital world. NFTs are unique digital tokens that represent ownership of a particular digital asset, such as an image, video, or music file. Each NFT is unique and cannot be replicated or duplicated, which means that it is easy to establish the originality and ownership of a digital asset. NFTs are stored on a blockchain, which is a distributed ledger that records all transactions and changes to the ownership of a digital asset. This makes it easy to track the ownership and history of a digital asset, which can be used to establish its provenance.

Here are five examples of how NFTs solve the problem of provenance in the digital world:

> Art: NFTs have become popular in the art world, where they are used to establish the ownership and provenance of digital art. NFTs can be used to verify the authenticity of a digital art piece, and the blockchain can be used to track its ownership and any changes made to it over time. For example, the artist Beeple sold a digital artwork for $69 million in March 2021, and the NFT used to represent the artwork established the ownership and authenticity of the piece.

Music: NFTs can be used to establish the ownership and provenance of music files, which are often subject to piracy and intellectual property theft. NFTs can be used to verify the ownership of a music file, and the blockchain can be used to track its usage and any changes made to it over time. For example, Kings of Leon became the first band to release an album as an NFT in March 2021, which established the ownership and authenticity of the album.

Gaming: NFTs are becoming popular in the gaming industry, where they can be used to establish the ownership and provenance of in-game assets, such as virtual real estate, characters, and items. NFTs can be used to verify the ownership of an in-game asset, and the blockchain can be used to track its usage and any changes made to it over time. For example, the game Axie Infinity allows players to own and trade NFTs representing in-game assets, which establishes the ownership and authenticity of the assets.

Real estate: NFTs can be used to establish the ownership and provenance of real estate assets, such as property deeds and contracts. NFTs can be used to verify the ownership of a real estate asset, and the blockchain can be used to track its ownership and any changes made to it over time.

Sports memorabilia: NFTs can be used to establish the ownership and provenance of sports memorabilia, such as trading cards, jerseys,

and equipment. NFTs can be used to verify the
authenticity of a sports memorabilia item, and the
blockchain can be used to track its ownership and
any changes made to it over time. For example,
the National Basketball Association (NBA) has
partnered with a company called NBA Top Shot to
sell NFTs representing digital collectibles, such as
game highlights and player cards, which establish
the ownership and authenticity of the collectibles.

Royalties

Royalties are a form of payment made to the owner of an intellectual
property right, typically in exchange for the use of that right. In the context
of music, for example, royalties are paid to songwriters and publishers
when their music is used in a variety of ways, such as when it is played on
the radio, streamed online, or included in a movie or TV show.

In the digital world, the concept of royalties is equally important,
if not more so. With the rise of digital media, it has become easier than
ever for people to create and distribute their own content, whether it be
music, videos, images, or other forms of digital art. However, this ease
of distribution has also created new challenges for creators, who must
now contend with issues like piracy, unauthorized use of their work, and
difficulty in tracking and enforcing their intellectual property rights.

One way that creators can address these challenges is by using
NFTs. NFTs are a type of digital asset that are stored on a blockchain, a
decentralized ledger that records transactions in a secure and transparent
way. When someone buys an NFT, they are essentially buying a unique
digital token that represents ownership of a particular piece of content,
such as a song, video, or artwork.

NFTs are designed to solve a number of problems that have long plagued the world of digital content, including the issue of royalties. Because NFTs are stored on a blockchain, they allow creators to establish ownership of their work in a way that is transparent and easily verifiable. This means that if someone wants to use a piece of content that is associated with an NFT, they will need to obtain permission from the owner and pay any required royalties.

To illustrate the concept of royalties and how NFTs can help solve the problem, let's look at five different examples:

> Music: A musician creates a new song and releases it on a streaming platform like Spotify. Because the song is associated with an NFT, the musician can ensure that they receive a share of the revenue generated from streams of the song, even if it is added to playlists or used in other contexts without their direct involvement.

> Art: An artist creates a digital artwork and sells it as an NFT. Because the ownership of the artwork is recorded on a blockchain, the artist can ensure that they receive a portion of any subsequent sales of the artwork, even if it is sold or traded multiple times.

> Video games: A game developer creates a new video game and distributes it through an online platform like Steam. By associating the game with an NFT, the developer can ensure that they receive a share of the revenue generated by the game, even if it is sold or distributed through other channels.

> Photography: A photographer takes a stunning photograph and licenses it for use on a website or in a magazine. By using an NFT to establish

ownership of the photograph, the photographer can ensure that they receive a royalty payment for each use of the photograph, whether it is used once or multiple times.

Writing: An author writes a new book and self-publishes it on a platform like Amazon. By associating the book with an NFT, the author can ensure that they receive a share of the revenue generated by sales of the book, even if it is sold or distributed through other channels.

Summary

In this chapter we discussed the rapid pace of technological innovation and its impact on various aspects of our lives. We highlighted how information technology has evolved from providing mere tools to do specific things for us to platforms that drive further innovations. The chapter emphasizes that the present era is characterized by pervasive digital engagement in almost every aspect of our lives. Despite this digital transformation, we identify a misalignment between the core attributes of the digital ecosystem and traditional economic value chains. Five critical attributes of the digital world are addressed: scarcity, ownership, authenticity, provenance, and royalties. The chapter delves into the significance of these attributes, discusses the challenges posed by the digital realm, and introduces non-fungible tokens (NFTs) as a solution that addresses these challenges. It examines how NFTs provide digital scarcity, unique ownership, authenticity verification, and provenance tracking and facilitate royalty payments in the digital domain. The introduction sets the stage for exploring the role of NFTs in reshaping the way we perceive and interact with digital assets.

CHAPTER 2

The Technology Behind NFTs

The technology which powers the creation, transfer, and use of NFTs is broadly known as either blockchain or distributed ledger technology in some circles. While Bitcoin was the first commonly used blockchain protocol, the technology has roots decades older than that. In this chapter we'll get familiar with the technology.

Blockchain Basics

The government of Estonia began using blockchain in 2008, a year before Bitcoin was launched. In fact, it can be argued that blockchain technology was invented by researchers Stuart Haber and W. Scott Stornetta when they published "How to Time-Stamp a Digital Document" in 1991.

At its core, blockchain technology is a decentralized and transparent ledger system that provides a secure and immutable record of time-stamped transactions. Blockchain allows for the creation of smart contracts, which are self-executing contracts with the terms of the agreement between buyer and seller being directly written into lines of code and run without requiring any human actions once the smart contract has been deployed. This technology enables trustless transactions, meaning that parties can transact with one another without the need for a trusted intermediary.

A blockchain is thus a distributed database that stores records of transactions across a network of computers. Each "block" in the chain contains a set of transactions – once a block is added to the chain, it cannot be altered or deleted. This ensures that the records on the blockchain are secure, transparent, and tamper-proof. Each blockchain uses what is called a "consensus mechanism" to add a block to the chain. These mechanisms ensure network users agree on the validity of each transaction.

There are a variety of different consensus mechanisms a blockchain can use. Examples include proof of work, proof of stake, and delegated proof of stake. Proof of work (PoW) is the consensus mechanism used by Bitcoin and is considered by many in the blockchain space to be the most secure one. The most common criticism of PoW is not based on its security, but its energy consumption; in a proof-of-work system, miners compete to solve complex mathematical problems in order to validate transactions and add new blocks to the blockchain, which can be an energy-intensive process in certain implementations.

Proof of stake (PoS) is another very popular consensus mechanism. It is the mechanism used by Ethereum, which transitioned from a PoW protocol on September 15, 2022. PoS does not require miners to solve complex problems, but instead relies on validators who hold and "stake" a certain amount of the "ledger-native token," or the token on which the blockchain runs, to validate transactions and add new blocks to the blockchain. For the Ethereum blockchain, the ledger-native token is ETH (Ethereum). Due to the lack of miners in a PoS ecosystem, it is much less energy intensive and often carries lower transaction fees.

One of the key features of blockchain technology is its immutability. Once a block has been added to the blockchain, altering or deleting it without being detected is impossible. Such changes are possible but require the consent of a majority of all block producers, which in a PoW system are the miners and in a PoS system are the validators. This ensures the integrity and security of the blockchain assuming it is mature enough to resist a "51% attack" whereby a malicious actor seizes control of over half the block producers, giving them the ability to edit the blockchain. This makes it an ideal technology for the creation and transfer of valuable digital assets, such as NFTs, on more mature networks.

However, immutability can also pose a challenge in situations where errors need to be corrected or transactions need to be reversed, such as in the case of a hack or criminal activity. Some blockchains such as Energi have been designed with this problem in mind and offer solutions, which are appealing for enterprise use cases, but these chains are relatively few in number.

That said, there has been a growing interest in the development of enterprise blockchain solutions in recent years. These solutions are designed to meet the needs of businesses and organizations and typically offer additional features such as permissioned access, scalability, and interoperability. Some of the leading enterprise blockchain solutions include Hyperledger Fabric, R3 Corda, and Quorum.

Thanks to the decentralized nature of these blockchains, enterprises which face risks from storing important data on centralized servers can mitigate these risks. Because the blockchain is stored across a network of computers rather than in a central location, it is highly resistant to attacks and tampering. This technology has sparked interest in sectors such as healthcare where institutions would rather not hold user data but still need to know about their customers – NFTs can serve a valuable role here by allowing patients to provide customized access to their health data to various providers.

Another widely regarded benefit of blockchain technology is transparency. All transactions are publicly recorded on the blockchain, meaning they are publicly visible and easily auditable. There are some exceptions with privacy chains such as Grin or Secret Network, but even in many of those chains a lot of data can be made natively public. This ensures that all parties in the network, or to a given transaction, have a clear and accurate view of what has taken place. This promotes trust between actors.

Also, despite the media barrage about hacks and security breaches, blockchain technology itself is highly secure. Flaws almost always come from poorly designed smart contracts which are then exploited to drain tokens. However, on-chain information and data are extremely hack resistant. Each block in the chain is cryptographically linked to the previous block, creating a secure and immutable record of transactions. This ensures that transactions cannot be altered or deleted without being detected, which helps prevent fraud.

This fraud prevention is one of the key benefits offered by blockchain technology. Since every transaction on a blockchain is verified by a vast network of nodes, the system is virtually tamper-proof unless a malicious actor manages to execute a 51% attack. The technology is also resistant to cyberattacks, as blockchains use advanced cryptographic techniques to protect against unauthorized access. Also, any discrepancies or irregularities can be quickly identified and investigated.

Another key benefit of blockchain technology is its ability to create trust. Since every transaction is verified and recorded on the blockchain, no trusted intermediaries are needed for transactions – escrows can be fully automated. This "cuts out the middleman" which can reduce costs and increase efficiency. It also means nobody can "cheat" or misallocate funds. For example, a nonprofit running a fundraiser using cryptocurrency cannot simply pocket donor money without spending it on the initiatives they promised to support.

Blockchains generally consist of five layers, each serving a different function. These layers are as follows:

1. Hardware layer

2. Network layer

3. Protocol layer

4. Middleware layer

5. Application layer

The hardware layer is the lowest layer. It is the physical infrastructure, consisting of physical components such as servers, storage devices, and miners, and other hardware depending on the specifics of the chain.

The network layer sits above the hardware layer and provides the underlying infrastructure for communication between nodes on the network, such as peer-to-peer networking, data propagation, and security.

The protocol layer is above the network layer and defines the rules and protocols that govern the operation of the network, such as consensus mechanisms, block validation, and transaction processing.

The middleware layer sits between the protocol layer and the application layer, providing the necessary infrastructure to support programs running on the chain. It includes protocols for data storage, messaging, and communication between different components of the network.

The application layer is the highest layer and is where users interact with the network and where applications are built. It includes the user interface, smart contracts, and decentralized applications (dApps). Most people using a blockchain only ever interface with this layer.

The security blockchain technology creates an environment for digital assets to flourish in ways they never could have with other technologies. Since past information cannot be easily altered, data cannot simply be copied and pasted, ownership can be verified, and intermediaries can be removed, blockchain can be an attractive option for businesses or other organizations looking to streamline operations and reduce costs. We will likely see more developments and an increasing number of use cases as the technology continues to develop. This is exemplified by the continued deployment of many different types of blockchains, each with their own specialized purposes.

There are several different types of blockchain networks, including public, private, and hybrid networks.

Public blockchain networks are open to anyone who wishes to participate in the network. These networks are decentralized and rely on a distributed network of nodes to validate transactions and add new blocks to the chain. Public networks, such as Bitcoin and Ethereum, are often referred to as permissionless networks, as anyone can participate in the network without the need for permission from a central authority.

Private blockchain networks, on the other hand, are restricted to a specific group of users, such as a company or organization. These networks are often referred to as permissioned networks, as participants must be granted permission to join the network by a central authority. Private networks offer several benefits over public networks, including increased privacy and control over network governance.

Hybrid blockchain networks combine elements of both public and private networks and are becoming increasingly popular for use in enterprise applications. These networks offer the benefits of both public and private networks, including decentralized trust, permissioned access, and increased security. Hybrid networks are often used in applications where privacy is important, but where the benefits of a public network are also desired, such as in supply chain management or identity verification.

In addition to public, private, and hybrid networks, there are also different types of consensus mechanisms that can be used to validate transactions on a blockchain. These mechanisms include the previously mentioned proof of work and proof-of-stake mechanisms, but there are many more. Each consensus mechanism has its own set of advantages and disadvantages and is suited to different types of blockchain networks and applications.

Let's take a more detailed look at some of the more popular consensus mechanisms:

> Proof of work (PoW): Proof of work is the original
> consensus mechanism used in blockchain
> technology and is still used by popular
> cryptocurrencies like Bitcoin. In PoW, miners
> compete to solve complex mathematical problems

in order to validate new blocks on the blockchain. The first miner to solve the problem is rewarded with newly minted cryptocurrency. While PoW is secure and decentralized, it is also energy-intensive and can lead to centralization of mining power.

Proof of stake (PoS): Proof of stake is an alternative to PoW that is designed to be more energy-efficient. In PoS, validators hold a stake in the blockchain and are chosen to validate new blocks based on the size of their stake. Validators are incentivized to act in the best interest of the network, as their stake can be slashed if they are found to be acting maliciously. PoS is often marketed as a more sustainable and environmentally friendly alternative to PoW. Ethereum is the most popular PoS blockchain.

Delegated proof of stake (DPoS): Delegated proof of stake is similar to PoS, but with a different approach to selecting validators. In DPoS, token holders vote for a limited number of delegates who are responsible for validating transactions on the blockchain. This approach is more centralized than PoW or PoS, but can lead to faster transaction processing times and lower energy consumption. An example of a DPoS blockchain is EOS, which offers zero transaction fees.

Proof of authority (PoA): Proof of authority is a consensus mechanism that relies on a small group of trusted validators to validate transactions on the blockchain. This approach is fast and efficient, but can be less secure and decentralized than other consensus mechanisms. Binance Smart Chain (BSC) uses a variant on the proof-of-authority model, called proof-of-staked authority.

Proof of history (PoH): Proof of history is a new consensus mechanism that is being developed by the Solana blockchain platform. PoH is designed to improve network scalability by enabling validators to precompute the order of transactions, rather than having to reach consensus on transaction order in real time.

The different types of blockchain networks offer unique advantages and are suited to different types of applications and use cases. Public networks are ideal for applications where decentralization and open access are important, while private networks offer increased control and privacy. Hybrid networks combine the best of both worlds, offering decentralized trust, permissioned access, and increased security. However, blockchains do come with some inherent disadvantages which vary depending on the specifics of each chain.

Addressing Obstacles

One of the primary challenges most blockchains face is scalability. As the level of activity on a blockchain network grows, the size of the blockchain also grows, making it increasingly difficult and time-consuming to process transactions. This can cause slower transaction times and higher transaction fees, particularly during periods of high network activity.

To address the issue of scalability, several solutions have been developed and implemented in different ways. These solutions include state channels, sidechains, and sharding. State channels and sidechains are both considered to be "Layer 2" solutions.

A Layer 2 solution is, in short, a blockchain built on top of another blockchain. Most Layer 2s are built on Ethereum, which is considered a Layer 1 because it is a base-layer blockchain. They allow for transactions to take place in a separate environment which are then posted to the Layer 1 chain. This reduces the load on the main blockchain and enables the improved performance.

State channels are a simple Layer 2 that enables two parties to transact with one another off the main blockchain. This can help to reduce the number of transactions on the main blockchain and improve scalability.

Sidechains are a type of off-chain solution that enables the creation of separate, parallel blockchains that are linked to the main blockchain. These sidechains can be used to process transactions that are not critical to the main blockchain, helping to improve overall network efficiency and scalability. This can help to reduce the load on the main blockchain, allowing it to process critical transactions more quickly and efficiently. Sidechain transactions are generally "rolled up" into a larger transaction which is then settled on the main chain.

One popular sidechain solution is the Polygon network, which is designed to address the issue of scalability in the Ethereum blockchain. The Polygon network is a Layer 2 scaling solution that is built on top of the Ethereum blockchain, enabling faster and cheaper transactions while still maintaining the benefits of the primary Ethereum network.

The Polygon network achieves this by using a combination of Plasma and PoS (proof-of-stake) technologies. This enables transactions to be processed in a separate blockchain that is linked to the Ethereum Mainnet. This helps reduce the load on the main Ethereum blockchain, allowing it to process critical transactions more quickly and efficiently. The Polygon network, like most blockchains modeled after Ethereum, supports the use of smart contracts written in the Solidity programming language.

Binance Smart Chain (BSC), also called BNB Chain, is another example of a successful sidechain solution. BSC is a blockchain network built on top of the Binance Chain, which is a high-performance blockchain that was designed specifically for the Binance exchange. BSC is compatible with the Ethereum Virtual Machine (EVM), which means that it supports the use of Ethereum-based smart contracts.

BSC was designed to address the scalability and transaction speed limitations of the Ethereum network. Like other sidechain solutions, BSC allows for faster and cheaper transactions by processing them off the main Ethereum blockchain. This is achieved through a system of validators, which are responsible for verifying and processing transactions on the BSC network.

One of the key features of BSC is that its transaction fees are significantly lower than those on the Ethereum network. For people and organizations who use BSC over Ethereum, this is almost always the reason they made that decision. The fees are lower because BSC uses its proof-of-staked authority (PoSA) consensus mechanism, which enables faster transaction processing times while still maintaining a sufficient degree of network security and decentralization.

BSC also supports a wide range of decentralized finance (DeFi) applications, including decentralized exchanges (DEXs), yield farming, and lending and borrowing protocols. These applications are all powered by smart contracts written in the Solidity programming language.

Sharding is a different solution to the scalability problem in blockchain networks which initially shows promise, though it has been subject to criticism. It is a technique used to improve the scalability and performance of blockchain networks by dividing the blockchain into smaller, more manageable segments called "shards," which can be processed independently. Each shard processes a subset of transactions, which allows for parallel processing and increased throughput, improving overall transaction processing times and network scalability.

One of the primary benefits of sharding is that it enables blockchain networks to scale horizontally, rather than vertically. This means that instead of relying on a single, monolithic blockchain to process all transactions, the network can be divided into smaller, more manageable pieces that can work together to process transactions in a more efficient manner.

With the launch of Ethereum 2.0, in an event also known as "The Merge," the network now includes a sharding solution known as the Beacon Chain. The Beacon Chain "merged" with the Ethereum Mainnet on September 15, 2022, coinciding with the transition of the Ethereum network from a PoW consensus mechanism to a PoS mechanism. The Beacon Chain coordinates the various shards in the Ethereum network and ensures that they are all working together in a secure and decentralized manner. This has helped to improve the scalability and efficiency of the network and has allowed for faster transaction processing times.

Sharding is not without flaws. For example, since each shard processes transactions independently, the security of the entire network can be compromised if a single shard is attacked successfully. A smaller number of nodes in each shard may make it easier for an attacker to gain control of a significant portion of the shard, potentially leading to double-spending or other malicious activities. Furthermore, the fact that nodes on sharded chains need not store the entire blockchain history means if one shard goes offline there can be delays or loss of data. It also increases network fragmentation, which can create unbalanced resource distribution and systemic inefficiency.

The use of sharding in Ethereum has been a significant step for the chain, as it demonstrates that this approach to improving network scalability can be both viable and effective. As a result, other blockchain projects may very well follow suit and explore the use of sharding in their own networks if the drawbacks are shown to be properly manageable.

Another blockchain project that is exploring the use of sharding is Zilliqa. Zilliqa is a high-throughput blockchain platform that uses sharding to improve network scalability and transaction processing times. The platform is designed to be fast, secure, and efficient and has already been used for a variety of applications, including payments, gaming, and digital advertising.

In addition to its sharding technology, Zilliqa also utilizes a unique consensus mechanism known as Practical Byzantine Fault Tolerance (PBFT). PBFT is well suited for permissioned blockchain networks, where the nodes are known and can be authenticated. Its major advantages are its resilience to Byzantine faults and finality of transactions, but it has limited scalability which Zilliqa has attempted to address through sharding.

Zilliqa also features a smart contract platform known as Scilla, which is designed to be more secure and developer-friendly than other smart contract languages. Scilla uses formal verification techniques to ensure that smart contracts are free from bugs and vulnerabilities, and it provides a clear and easy-to-use programming language for developers.

The foundations of blockchain technology make assets like NFTs possible, but one other core component is the use of cryptography. Without cryptography, these protocols and the assets on them would be completely useless.

Cryptography and Encryption

Cryptography is a fundamental aspect of blockchain technology that ensures the security and authenticity of transactions. It employs various techniques, such as digital signatures, to confirm that transactions are genuinely initiated by the claiming party. In the blockchain, each user has a public and private key pair. The private key remains secret and is used to create digital signatures, which can only be decrypted using the user's public key, accessible to everyone.

The creation and transfer of digital signatures, which users employ to verify transaction authenticity and prevent tampering or forgery, is the primary use case for cryptography when it comes to NFTs. Digital signatures are created using cryptographic techniques involving a public and private key pair for each user on the blockchain, providing a secure and reliable method to verify authenticity and ownership.

Users generate digital signatures when initiating transactions, employing their private key to create a signature that includes transaction details. This signature is sent with the transaction to the blockchain network, allowing other network users to use the sender's public key to verify the digital signature and confirm the sender's identity.

Digital signatures are created by applying a cryptographic hash function to the NFT data and encrypting the resulting hash value using the private key. The encrypted hash value and public key are stored on the blockchain as a digital signature, ensuring the signature's uniqueness to the NFT and its inability to verify any other NFT's authenticity.

These techniques are integral to smart contracts as well as NFTs – it ensures their uniqueness, authenticity, and value. It verifies ownership and transfer of NFTs, preventing replication or counterfeiting. Without it, NFTs would lose their functional value.

This approach also enables user anonymity while allowing blockchain transaction participation. The public key verifies transaction authenticity without disclosing the sender's identity, essential for transferring sensitive financial or personal information while maintaining privacy and anonymity.

The smart contracts involved in the creation and use of NFTs ensure that execution is secure and tamper-proof. When an NFT is created, it is assigned a unique identifier that is stored on the blockchain network. This identifier is generated using a cryptographic hash function, which is a mathematical algorithm that takes in data and produces a fixed-size output.

The use of a hash function ensures that the NFT is unique and cannot be replicated or counterfeited. It also enables users to verify the ownership of an NFT by comparing the hash value of the NFT with the hash value stored on the blockchain. If the hash values match, then the NFT is authentic and owned by the user who claims to own it.

The most common hash function in blockchain is the SHA-256 (Secure Hash Algorithm 256-bit), which is a widely recognized and secure cryptographic algorithm. SHA-256 takes an input of any length and produces a fixed-length 256-bit output, which is uniquely generated based on the input data.

While SHA-256 is the most commonly used hash function in blockchain technology, there are other hash algorithms that could be used in NFTs as well. One alternative is the SHA-3 (Secure Hash Algorithm 3) algorithm, which was developed by the National Institute of Standards and Technology (NIST) and introduced in 2015. Like SHA-256, SHA-3 is a cryptographic hash function that produces a fixed-length output. However, it uses a different algorithm than SHA-256, which makes it less vulnerable to certain types of attacks.

Another alternative hash function is BLAKE2, which was introduced in 2012 and is a faster and more efficient alternative to SHA-256. BLAKE2 is a family of hash functions that includes BLAKE2b and BLAKE2s, which are optimized for 64-bit and 32-bit platforms, respectively. BLAKE2 is also highly parallelizable, which makes it well suited for use in GPUs and other hardware accelerators.

Even though SHA-256 is the most widely used blockchain hash function, alternative algorithms could be useful in certain scenarios, such as when speed, efficiency, or resistance to certain types of attacks are important considerations. Ultimately, the choice of hash function will depend on the specific requirements of the NFT application and the desired balance between security, efficiency, and other factors.

Several blockchains have implemented alternative hash algorithms beyond SHA-256 to secure their networks and improve their efficiency. Some examples include the following:

> Ethereum: Ethereum uses a hash algorithm called Keccak-256 to secure its network. Keccak-256 was selected through a competition held by the National

Institute of Standards and Technology (NIST) to create a new hash function standard called SHA-3. Keccak-256 produces a 256-bit output and is known for its high security and efficiency.

Ripple: Ripple is a blockchain platform that uses the hash algorithm SHA-512 in its consensus protocol to provide high security and efficiency. SHA-512 produces a 512-bit output and is considered more secure than SHA-256.

Zcash: Zcash is a privacy-focused cryptocurrency that uses the hash algorithm Equihash for its proof-of-work consensus protocol. Equihash is a memory-intensive algorithm that requires significant amounts of memory to solve, which makes it resistant to ASIC mining and ensures a more decentralized network.

Grin: Grin is a privacy-focused cryptocurrency that uses the hash algorithm MimbleWimble to ensure the privacy of transactions. MimbleWimble combines multiple cryptographic techniques, including elliptic curve cryptography (ECC), confidential transactions, and Pedersen commitments, to provide a high degree of privacy and security.

These are just a few examples of blockchains that use alternative hash algorithms to secure their networks. Over time, there will almost certainly be further innovations in hash algorithms and other security measures to improve the efficiency, security, and privacy of blockchain networks.

When an NFT is created, its unique digital content is hashed using the relevant algorithm. This creates a unique digital fingerprint of the

NFT, which is stored on the blockchain along with other information such as the owner's public key (their wallet address), the date of creation, and the smart contract governing the NFT. Because the hash function is deterministic, the same input data will always produce the same output hash value. This means that the hash value can be used to verify the authenticity and ownership of an NFT.

The hash value of an NFT can be compared with the hash value stored on the blockchain to ensure that the NFT is authentic and has not been tampered with. Because the hash value is unique to the NFT, it cannot be used to create a counterfeit or duplicate NFT. Even small changes in the digital content of the NFT will result in a completely different hash value, making it effectively impossible to create a counterfeit or duplicate NFT that matches the hash value of the original.

The use of a hash function in NFTs is a critical component of their authenticity and value. It enables users to verify that an NFT is unique, authentic, and owned by the user who claims to own it. This is important in many sectors, but particularly in the world of digital art, where the value of an NFT is often based on its uniqueness and authenticity. Without a reliable way to verify the authenticity of an NFT, it would be difficult to establish its value or prevent counterfeiting.

When a user wants to verify the ownership of an NFT, they can compare the digital signature stored on the blockchain with the digital signature created from the NFT data. This process involves applying the same hash function to the NFT data and then decrypting the digital signature using the public key. If the decrypted value matches the hash value, then the NFT is authentic and owned by the user who claims to own it.

All of this, from the digital signatures to the hashing algorithms used to the fingerprint of each NFT, ensures the authenticity and ownership of each digital asset. They provide a secure and reliable way to verify the ownership of NFTs and work to prevent counterfeiting and fraud in the NFT market. As NFTs continue to mature and see additional use cases.

Additional innovations beyond the use of digital signatures and presently employed cryptographic techniques will almost certainly improve security and authenticity of NFTs.

Another crucial aspect of blockchain security, and the security of NFTs by proxy, is encryption. Without encryption, sensitive information such as wallet addresses and private keys would be exposed to unauthorized access, potentially leading to the loss of valuable NFTs or even entire wallets. There would be no use cases for blockchain technology without secure encryption to ensure that only authorized parties are able to access this sensitive information, providing a critical layer of protection against theft and unauthorized access.

In fact, encryption is a critical aspect of security in all areas of digital technology. Not only that, but it is increasingly important as encryption-breaking techniques and the raw processing power behind them continue to increase. Developers and users alike must remain vigilant in their efforts to ensure that encryption is properly implemented and maintained to keep all digital assets secure and protected from theft and fraud.

One example of a blockchain that places a strong emphasis on encryption is the privacy-focused blockchain, Monero. Monero uses a unique encryption technique called ring signatures, which obfuscates the source of a transaction by allowing multiple users to sign a transaction without revealing which user actually initiated it. This makes it exceedingly difficult for anyone to trace transactions on the Monero blockchain, ensuring a high level of privacy and security for users. To date, nobody has successfully traced a Monero transaction without compromising a device used to initiate it.

Zcash also uses encryption extensively. It uses zero-knowledge proofs (ZKPs) to encrypt transaction information, including the sender's address, the recipient's address, and the amount of the transaction. This allows users to transact on the blockchain without revealing any information about themselves or their transactions, ensuring a high level of privacy and security.

Zero-knowledge proofs are a type of cryptographic proof that allows one party to prove to another party that a statement is true, without revealing any additional information beyond the truth of the statement itself. This is achieved by using mathematical algorithms that enable a proof to be constructed without revealing the underlying data used in the proof.

The zero-knowledge proof protocol used by Zcash is called zk-SNARKs (zero-knowledge succinct non-interactive argument of knowledge), which is one of the most powerful applications of zero-knowledge proofs. Zk-SNARKs are a type of zero-knowledge proof that allows for the verification of a transaction without revealing any of the transaction details or the identities of the parties involved. Its use is not limited to Zcash and is also employed by Pirate Chain and Ethereum among others, though implementation is currently rather limited on Ethereum.

Zk-SNARKs work by using a mathematical algorithm to create a succinct proof of the validity of a transaction. The proof is then shared with the network, which can verify the proof without knowing any of the underlying details of the transaction. This makes zk-SNARKs a powerful tool for ensuring privacy and confidentiality in blockchain transactions, as they enable transactions to be validated without revealing any sensitive information.

One of the primary use cases for zk-SNARKs is in the creation of private blockchains, where transactions need to be validated without revealing any sensitive information. For example, in a supply chain management system, a private blockchain could be used to track the movement of goods from one location to another. By using zk-SNARKs, each transaction in the supply chain could be validated without revealing the details of the goods being transported or the parties involved in the transaction.

Zero-knowledge proofs and zk-SNARKs can be applied to NFTs in several ways.

First, zero-knowledge proofs can be used to prove ownership of an NFT without revealing any sensitive information. For example, a user could prove that they own an NFT without revealing their wallet address or any other identifying information. This can help to protect the privacy and security of NFT owners.

Second, zero-knowledge proofs can be used to prove the authenticity of an NFT without revealing any details about the NFT itself. For example, a user could prove that an NFT is genuine without revealing any information about the digital content or the specific NFT being verified. This can help to prevent counterfeit NFTs from entering the market and ensure that buyers are purchasing authentic NFTs.

Third, zk-SNARKs can be used to enable private transactions of NFTs. This means that users can buy, sell, and trade NFTs without revealing any details about the transaction to the public. This can help to protect the privacy and security of NFT owners, particularly in cases where large sums of money are involved.

Zero-knowledge proofs and zk-SNARKs are powerful tools. By enabling privacy, security, and authenticity, these cryptographic techniques can help to improve the overall trust and value of NFTs.

This makes them a valuable tool for a wide range of applications, from supply chain management to authentication to proving provenance. For example, a company that produces high-end luxury goods could use NFTs secured with ZKPs to ensure the authenticity of their products and prevent counterfeiting. Each product could be associated with a unique NFT that contains information about the product's origin, production, and distribution. The NFT would be secured using ZKPs to protect all sensitive information from unauthorized access.

As the product changes hands, the NFT can be transferred between different parties, such as distributors, retailers, and customers. Each transfer would be recorded on the blockchain, ensuring a transparent and immutable record of the product's movement.

The use of NFTs secured by zero-knowledge proofs can also help to reduce the amount of paperwork involved in buying and selling art. Currently, buyers and sellers must rely on paper-based documentation to verify the authenticity and provenance of an artwork. This can be time-consuming and costly and may not provide a complete picture of an artwork's history. By using NFTs, buyers and sellers can access a complete and verifiable record of an artwork's history in a more efficient and cost-effective manner.

ZKP-secured NFTs used in this way would provide several benefits to both the company and the consumers. For the company, it would provide an additional layer of security for their products, helping to prevent counterfeiting and protect their brand reputation. For consumers, it would provide a way to verify the authenticity and quality of the products they are purchasing, helping to build trust in the supply chain and reduce the risk of fraud.

Encryption thus plays a crucial role in protecting sensitive information in NFTs and blockchain networks. Without proper encryption, the security and integrity of the blockchain ecosystem would be compromised, and users' personal and financial data would be at risk of being exposed to malicious actors. That said, it's important that all such encryption is appropriately applied to all relevant transactions and smart contracts.

Smart Contracts

Smart contracts are created using programming languages specifically designed for the blockchain, such as Solidity for Ethereum and around 90% of all other EVM-compatible blockchains. In addition to being commonly used to automate business processes, they also are a key feature of NFTs, decentralized applications (dApps), and decentralized autonomous organizations (DAOs).

As for how a smart contract governs NFTs, when an NFT is created, a smart contract is deployed on the blockchain to specify the ownership and transfer rights of the NFT. Since this smart contract is stored on the blockchain, it can be executed automatically whenever the NFT is bought or sold, ensuring that ownership is transferred securely and transparently.

Smart contracts are designed to be trustless, meaning that they operate without the need for a trusted third party to enforce the terms of the agreement. The cryptography involved ensures that the execution of the contract is secure and tamper-proof. Since smart contracts are also immutable, once they are deployed, the terms of the agreement cannot be changed. This means NFTs cannot be simply reassigned or altered without going through the predefined rules of the smart contract.

The ability of smart contracts to automate processes is extensive and provides many benefits pertaining to NFTs. For example, in the art industry, a smart contract can be used to ensure that artists receive royalties every time an NFT of their artwork is resold. The smart contract can be programmed to automatically transfer a percentage of the sale price to the artist's account whenever the artwork is sold, without the need for manual intervention.

Suppose an artist creates a digital artwork and mints it as an NFT on a blockchain platform. They can then specify the terms of sale in a smart contract, including the percentage of the sale price that they want to receive as a royalty payment whenever the NFT is resold.

This smart contract is then executed automatically whenever a relevant NFT is sold, and the specified percentage of the sale price is transferred to the artist's account as a royalty payment. Because the smart contract is stored on the blockchain, it is transparent and cannot be altered or manipulated by any party. This ensures that the artist receives the appropriate compensation for their work, and that ownership is properly transferred.

Similarly, the disintermediation provided by smart contracts comes into play with NFTs as a way to increase efficiency. By automating the terms of a contract, smart contracts eliminate the need for traditional intermediaries, such as banks and lawyers, which can reduce transaction costs and increase efficiency. Since these smart contracts are stored on the blockchain, and thus are immutable and tamper-proof, they provide an additional layer of security and transparency to business transactions which leverage them.

However, smart contracts are not perfect; they have limitations. They are only as good as the code that defines them. If there is an error in the code, it can lead to unintended consequences and security vulnerabilities. Such vulnerabilities can be exploited by attackers to steal funds or cause other damage. Since NFTs are valued for being unique digital assets, any errors in the code of the smart contract governing them can have significant consequences, including financial ones.

One high-profile example of a smart contract hack occurred in 2016 with the decentralized autonomous organization (DAO). The DAO was a decentralized venture capital fund built on the Ethereum blockchain that raised over $150 million from investors. However, a vulnerability in the smart contract code was exploited, resulting in the theft of one-third of the funds, or around $50 million at the time. This incident highlighted the importance of properly auditing and testing smart contract code to prevent such vulnerabilities.

Another example is the Poly Network hack, which occurred in August 2021. Poly Network is a cross-chain DeFi protocol that facilitates the exchange of tokens across multiple blockchains. The hackers exploited a vulnerability in the smart contract code, allowing them to steal approximately $600 million worth of cryptocurrency. However, the hackers eventually returned the funds after negotiations with Poly Network and the wider cryptocurrency community. This incident underscored the importance of security in DeFi protocols and the need for continuous auditing and testing of smart contracts.

The fact that some situations require judgment calls, moral or ethical considerations, or other circumstances which need a human "in-the-loop" to make a determination restricts the use of smart contracts in a lot of scenarios. Smart contracts are executed automatically and are unable to adapt to changing circumstances, which can be problematic if circumstances change unexpectedly or if there are unforeseen contingencies that were not accounted for in the original contract. Additionally, smart contracts may not be able to handle complex business logic, which may require human intervention to resolve.

For example, smart contracts may not be suitable for complex legal agreements. This would include those involving intellectual property or licensing agreements, as these types of agreements often require human interpretation and negotiation. It is possible that smart contract developers might fail to account for all the possible scenarios and contingencies that could arise in such agreements prior to their deployment, even with the assistance of AI.

Smart contracts may also not be suitable for transactions that require dispute resolution or mediation. In the case of a dispute between two parties over the terms of a smart contract, there may not be a clear mechanism for resolving the dispute within the terms of the contract. This could result in a situation where the parties are unable to reach a resolution, leading to possible financial loss and or even legal disputes.

Furthermore, smart contracts may not be suited to handle transactions that involve physical goods or services. It is distinctly likely that a given smart contract may be unable to verify the quality or authenticity of a physical product, which is an important consideration for industries such as food or pharmaceuticals. In these cases, there may be a need for human intervention to ensure that the terms of the contract are being met and that the physical product is of the expected quality.

It's important to carefully consider the suitability of smart contracts for a given transaction or agreement. While they offer many benefits in terms of efficiency and transparency, there are certain limitations and potential risks that must be taken into account before deciding to use this technology.

Smart contract developers must be diligent in identifying and addressing potential security vulnerabilities in their code to ensure that it is secure and free from errors. One key step in this process is to undergo rigorous testing and auditing of the smart contract code by independent third-party auditors who specialize in blockchain security. These auditors will assess the smart contract's code for vulnerabilities and recommend changes that can improve its security.

Auditing a smart contract involves a thorough analysis of the code to ensure that it is secure, efficient, and functioning as intended. The process typically involves several steps, including the following:

1. Static analysis: This involves reviewing the code for potential vulnerabilities and security flaws, such as buffer overflows, race conditions, and integer overflows.

2. Dynamic analysis: This involves testing the code to ensure that it functions as intended and that there are no bugs or logical errors.

3. Code review: This involves a human expert reviewing the code to ensure that it follows best practices, is well organized, and is easy to read and understand.

4. Penetration testing: This involves attempting to hack or exploit the smart contract to identify any weaknesses or vulnerabilities that could be exploited by an attacker.

5. Risk analysis: This involves assessing the potential risks associated with the smart contract, such as the likelihood of a security breach or the potential impact of a vulnerability.

6. Documentation review: This involves reviewing the documentation for the smart contract to ensure that it accurately describes its intended behavior and any limitations or risks associated with its use.

The goal of auditing a smart contract is to identify and remediate any vulnerabilities or flaws that could be exploited by an attacker. It is important to conduct regular audits throughout the development process, as well as after deployment, to ensure that the smart contract remains secure and effective over time.

Smart contract safeguards are mechanisms put in place to prevent or mitigate potential risks associated with the execution of smart contracts. One common safeguard is the use of circuit breakers. A circuit breaker is a software mechanism that pauses the execution of a smart contract in the event of an error or vulnerability. This allows developers to investigate and fix the issue before allowing the smart contract to resume execution.

Another safeguard is the use of multisignature wallets. Multisignature wallets require multiple parties to sign off on a transaction before it can be executed, which can prevent unauthorized or fraudulent transactions. This is particularly useful for transactions involving large amounts of value.

Other smart contract safeguards include the use of time locks, which delay the execution of a smart contract until a specified time or date. Time locks can be useful for transactions that require a waiting period before execution, such as the release of funds after a certain condition has been met. Another safeguard is the use of access controls, which restrict the execution of a smart contract to authorized parties only. This can prevent unauthorized access or tampering with the smart contract.

It develops also important for smart contract developers to use standard and widely accepted coding practices and to follow best practices for smart contract development. This includes following secure coding guidelines, using secure programming languages, and regularly updating the code to address any new vulnerabilities that may arise.

In cases where smart contracts cannot fully automate certain processes or where there may be ambiguity in the contract terms, incorporating human oversight or dispute resolution mechanisms can help ensure fair and transparent transactions.

One mechanism for ensuring fair and transparent transactions is to implement a dispute resolution process. This process can be built into the smart contract and can involve a neutral third-party arbitrator who is responsible for resolving any disputes that arise. The arbitrator can review the terms of the contract and any relevant data or evidence to determine the outcome of the dispute. This mechanism can be particularly useful in cases where the terms of the contract are ambiguous or require human judgment, such as in cases where there is a dispute over the ownership of an NFT.

It is important for developers to carefully consider the use of human oversight and dispute resolution mechanisms in their smart contracts, as they can add complexity and potential costs to the contract execution process. However, in cases where the potential risks and consequences of errors or disputes are significant, these mechanisms can provide an important layer of protection for all parties involved.

One other important aspect of many smart contracts is the concept of oracles. An oracle refers to a trusted third-party service or entity that provides external information to the smart contract.

Smart contracts operate within the blockchain ecosystem, which means that they have no access to external data sources, such as real-world events or data feeds. Oracles are used to provide that sort of data to the smart contract, allowing it to execute predefined actions based on the information received.

Oracles can operate using various types of external data, such as market prices, weather data, or sports scores. They can also be used to verify the outcome of specific events, such as the delivery of goods in a supply chain or the occurrence of a specific condition in an insurance contract.

Oracles can augment the functionality of smart contracts by allowing them to be programmed to execute actions based on external events and data. This means that smart contracts can be designed to operate in real-world situations that require real-time data, such as derivatives markets or sports betting. With oracles, smart contracts can be executed autonomously without the need for human intervention, making them more efficient.

However, oracles do introduce an element of trust into the smart contract ecosystem. As they are third-party services, there is a risk that they may provide inaccurate or biased data. This could compromise the integrity of the smart contract. Mitigating the risks this can pose can require carefully selecting and auditing the oracles intended for use to ensure that they are trustworthy and reliable.

Beyond the data-related risks, using an oracle can also introduce additional security risks. One of the main risks is that the oracle itself may be subject to manipulation or corruption. This in turn can introduce more data-related risks, though this time the risk comes from deliberate malicious actions rather than merely biased or incorrect data – attackers who compromise an oracle can cause it to send false information to the smart contract which triggers the execution of code that should not have run. This can be a vector to drain a smart contract of assets held within it.

In addition, the use of an oracle can also introduce vulnerabilities in the smart contract code itself. If the smart contract is not designed to handle unexpected or incorrect data from the oracle, it may execute incorrectly or even crash. Such events may be unrecoverable and lead to major losses, financial or otherwise.

Furthermore, oracles can also potentially compromise the privacy of the data being used in the smart contract. If the oracle has access to sensitive data, such as personal information or financial data, there is a risk that this data could be leaked or misused.

To mitigate these risks, it is important to carefully select and vet the oracle used in a smart contract and to implement appropriate security measures, such as data encryption and verification mechanisms, to protect against potential attacks. It is also important for the smart contract to be designed in a way that enables it to handle unexpected or incorrect data from the oracle. Contingency plans should be included within the code to handle any security breaches or other unexpected eventualities.

In general, though, it is considered a security best practice to avoid the use of oracles wherever possible due to the myriad risks they introduce. Sometimes they cannot be avoided when a blockchain-based solution is being developed, but often there are workarounds. Business leaders who seek to use NFTs as a part of their operations or service offerings need to know about these risks so they can perform an adequate cost-benefit analysis.

Such leaders must have at least some level of familiarity with smart contracts like what has been described here to avoid taking unnecessary risks, mistaking their capabilities, or making poor business decisions. Since blockchain tokens, including NFTs, are a form of smart contract, the foundations of this technology are critical to have when considering whether to implement such solutions.

Recall that smart contracts are self-executing contracts with the terms of the agreement written directly into code. They operate without the need for a trusted third party to enforce the terms of the agreement, and they automate business processes by executing code automatically based on predetermined conditions. This can be particularly advantageous in a variety of circumstances where automation is important.

As it relates to NFTs, smart contracts are used in the creation and transfer thereof, as well as to specify ownership and other relevant details. They can also be programmed to ensure that artists and creators are fairly compensated for their work via royalty protocols, which automatically transfer a percentage of the amount of a sale to the artist's account whenever the NFT is sold on a compliant platform, but this is just one of many applications of this technology.

However, smart contracts are not without their drawbacks. Blockchain engineers should rigorously test and audit the code to ensure that it is not subject to exploits and incorporates the latest best practices. Implementing safeguards such as circuit breakers can help, but as with any Internet-enabled solution, there is no silver bullet – vigilance is required.

Another potential issue with smart contracts is their inability to adapt to changing circumstances or unforeseen contingencies that were not accounted for in the original contract. Thankfully, smart contracts are generally "upgradable" which simply means they can be edited to fix issues uncovered, but retaining this ability generally reduces the trust a community of users has in the project as the developers could "rug pull" the project by changing the smart contracts in ways that harm the users but benefit the developers.

To address this, many projects "renounce" their smart contracts after deploying them to the blockchain. This simply means that the creators no longer have any control over the contract and are unable to make any future changes. Of course, this also means that any flaws or errors discovered later cannot be fixed.

Developers need to account for these decisions when creating their smart contracts. They may need to incorporate human oversight or dispute resolution mechanisms in certain cases to ensure that transactions are executed fairly and transparently. This may include using an oracle if it can be done securely, or employing some other trusted third party to verify the accuracy of data used in the smart contract. One approach that is increasingly common is to implement a DAO, which enables the community to make or approve changes to the smart contracts, but this is also fraught with concern.

Overall, smart contracts have significant potential for automating business processes, improving transparency and security, and ensuring fair compensation for artists and creators. However, they also pose risks and limitations that must be carefully considered and mitigated through rigorous testing, standard coding practices, and the incorporation of safeguards. As the NFT market continues to grow, the importance of developers and businesses alike understanding the potential benefits and risks of smart contracts continues to grow, as does the need to incorporate them effectively in their operations.

Summary

There are many different blockchains out there, and each blockchain is structured differently so as to be optimized for specific purposes. Understanding the benefits and drawbacks of each consensus mechanism, approach to decentralization, level of permissiveness, and more is crucial for business leaders trying to identify an appropriate chain for their use case.

While possessing a deep knowledge of details like the differences between a "Layer 1" and a "Layer 2" or higher blockchain, the specifics of how each individual consensus mechanism works, and how each ledger approaches encryption are not critical to making a decision on where to go, it is all helpful information to have. A more comprehensive understanding of these attributes can help optimize a decision when multiple blockchains meet the basic requirements.

One thing that decision makers *must* understand is how a chain handles smart contracts. Smart contracts are the core of any blockchain's ability to address a business need – tokens are smart contracts, NFTs are smart contracts, logical processes are smart contracts, and everything that runs on a blockchain uses smart contracts. Almost everything built on a blockchain is built using smart contracts.

Making sure the smart contract logic is understandable by your developers and that they grasp the coding language is a core need when selecting a chain. A developer who only knows Ethereum's Solidity will be at home on chains like Polygon or BNB Chain but have major difficulties coding on Flow or Polkadot which use other languages.

Different languages are optimized for different purposes, too. Selecting the wrong blockchain may impair your ability to deliver a product or service. This and other things such as the transaction fees and built-in privacy functions are among the key considerations when considering where to deploy any blockchain-driven project such as those using NFTs.

Another critical point is understanding the ecosystem which currently exists on the chain being considered, including which wallets support the chain and what marketplaces or other gateways already exist on it. The next chapter goes into greater detail on this subject.

CHAPTER 3

Creating and Selling NFTs

Now that we have covered the specifics of how blockchain technology works, and specifically how it powers NFTs, the next most important topic is the creation and sale or distribution of those NFTs. For NFTs to serve any purpose, they must be created and put out into the world so people can make use of them.

While there are many factors to be considered throughout this process, one of the most important ones is the characteristics of the NFTs one intends to create. It's also important to consider how the eventual holders of those NFTs will actually hold them, which means thinking about wallets, and how to get those NFTs into their hands, which is usually by selling them.

Characteristics

When creating an NFT, the first step is to determine the aspects that will make your NFT unique and valuable. This could be anything from a piece of artwork or a collectible card to a tweet or a virtual real estate property. The key is to ensure that the NFT has qualities that set it apart from other digital assets, and that these qualities are reflected in its design and metadata.

A. Bouzid et al., *NFTs for Business*, https://doi.org/10.1007/978-1-4842-9777-3_3

The aspects or variables of an NFT can vary greatly depending on the type of digital asset being represented.

Variables

In general, the variables of an NFT can be categorized into two main types: intrinsic and extrinsic.

Intrinsic Variables

These variables refer to the inherent qualities of the NFT itself. For example, in the case of a piece of artwork, intrinsic variables might include the artist's signature, the date it was created, the medium used, the dimensions, and any special techniques or materials used. For a virtual real estate property, intrinsic variables might include the location of the property, the size of the property, and any special features or amenities.

An example of NFTs which derive their value from intrinsic variables is the popular CryptoPunks NFT collection; each NFT has a unique 8-bit pixelated design that makes it easily identifiable and collectible. Another example is the Bored Ape Yacht Club NFT collection, where each NFT features a different illustration of a cartoon ape, with unique accessories and background elements.

Extrinsic Variables

On the other hand, these variables refer to external factors that contribute to the value or uniqueness of the NFT. For example, if the artwork was created by a well-known artist, this could increase its value. Similarly, if the virtual real estate property is located in a popular virtual world, this could increase its value and desirability.

For instance, in the NBA Top Shot NFT collection, each NFT represents a specific basketball moment, such as a dunk or a three-point shot, and has a limited-edition number that indicates its rarity. In the case of the

Beeple Everydays collection, the extrinsic value comes from the fact that it was the first NFT collection to be sold at a major auction house, Christie's, and that it was sold for a record-breaking sum of $69 million.

Some NFT collections attempt to increase their value over time by adding extrinsic value. Bored Ape Yacht Club is one example of this – Bored Apes creator Yuga Labs continues to develop new ways in which owners of Bored Apes can use them, such as avatars in their Otherside metaverse and access passes to special events.

Utility

Another variable to consider is the utility of the NFT. While some NFTs are purely collectible, many others have functional utility within a particular ecosystem or platform. For example, some gaming NFTs can be used as in-game items or currency, while others may be used as access keys to certain areas or features within a virtual world. Creators may want to consider how they can add functional utility to their NFTs to increase their value and appeal.

Utility can be considered as an extrinsic variable for an NFT. This is because the utility of an NFT is not inherent to the asset itself, but rather is derived from its use or purpose within a particular ecosystem or platform. In other words, the value of an NFT with functional utility depends on external factors and how it is integrated and utilized within a particular context.

For example, a gaming NFT may have functional utility within a particular game or virtual world, but this utility is dependent on the game or world in which it is used. The NFT itself does not have inherent functional utility without the context of the game or world. Similarly, an NFT that provides access to certain features or content within a platform has utility within that platform, but this utility is not intrinsic to the NFT itself.

For an example of a utility NFT, we can look again at NBA's Top Shot, where NFTs are used to represent digital collectibles in the form of basketball game highlights. These NFTs have both intrinsic and extrinsic value, with their functional utility being the ability to participate in fantasy sports games and access exclusive content and events.

Another example is the use of NFTs as access keys to exclusive content or events within a virtual world. For example, Decentraland, a virtual world built on the Ethereum blockchain, allows users to buy and sell NFTs that serve as tickets to exclusive virtual events and experiences.

In addition, some NFTs can be used as in-game items or currency, adding functional utility to the collectible asset. This is the case in many blockchain-based games, such as Axie Infinity and The Sandbox, where NFTs can be used as in-game assets and traded on decentralized marketplaces.

The inclusion of functional utility in an NFT can increase its appeal and value, as it provides a tangible benefit beyond just ownership of a collectible asset. Aspiring NFT creators would do well to consider the potential use cases for their NFTs and how they can add functional utility to attract a wider range of buyers and increase the long-term value of their NFTs.

Additional Variable Functions

Other aspects or variables of an NFT might include its rarity, its history, and its provenance.

Rarity refers to the scarcity of the NFT, which is generally considered to increase its value. History and provenance refer to the chain of ownership and the authentication of NFTs, which are also often considered to increase their value and ensure authenticity. This is by no means guaranteed though; bad provenance can certainly *decrease* value.

Rarity/scarcity is one of the most common factors used by NFT creators to try and increase their value. It creates a sense of exclusivity. To achieve this, creators can limit the number of NFTs in a collection, or create unique one-of-a-kind NFTs. This often called a "one of one." Scarcity can also be achieved by releasing NFTs in limited editions, with each edition having a fixed number of NFTs available for purchase.

Almost every NFT collection attempts to use the concept of rarity to increase value. Examples include the CryptoKitties NFT collection, in which each NFT represents a unique virtual cat with its own set of attributes, such as fur color and eye shape. Some of these cats are rarer than others, and collectors are willing to pay a premium for them. In the case of the World of Women NFT collection, each NFT represents a unique illustration of a female character, with some of them being rarer than others due to their unique features or backstory.

Keep in mind that as with provenance, rarity does not automatically increase value. If an NFT has no other value other than the fact that it is rare, that does not mean it will be inherently valuable. Many creators forget this and create collections that feature rarity thinking this will make them worth more, only to discover that nobody cares because there is no other value.

This brings us to another potentially valuable aspect of an NFT: historical significance. For example, the first tweet ever sent by Twitter CEO Jack Dorsey was turned into an NFT and sold for $2.9 million, with the historical significance of the tweet adding to its value. Another example is the first NFT ever created, which was sold for $1.5 million due to its historical significance and its role in establishing the NFT market.

Keep in mind though that this type of value is very dependent on the market and buyers' sentiment. The Jack Dorsey first tweet NFT may have sold for $2.9 million in March 2021, but was only able to fetch a top bid of $277 in April 2022 when it was put up for sale again.

There are multiple instances where NFTs have been minted that drew upon historically significant works or events outside the digital realm as well. The José Napoleón Duarte collection represents the body of work from the former president of El Salvador, with each NFT representing ownership of an authenticated reproduction of Duarte's works, speeches, and more by his estate.

Another important consideration when creating an NFT is its potential for interactivity. Unlike traditional physical artwork, NFTs can be designed to incorporate interactive elements such as animations, sound effects, and other multimedia components. This can add value and uniqueness to an NFT, as well as provide a more engaging and immersive experience for collectors and buyers. Bored Apes are a good example of NFTs that include components of interactivity – Snoop Dogg and Eminem even made a music video starring their Bored Apes.

Creators must take caution when creating secondary or derivative works from an NFT though: the creation and ownership of NFTs do not necessarily confer the copyright or intellectual property rights to the underlying artwork or asset. Copyright laws still apply, and it is crucial to ensure that all necessary permissions have been obtained before creating and selling an NFT. It is also important to consider the potential for plagiarism or copyright infringement when selling and distributing NFTs.

When Yuga Labs created the Bored Ape Yacht Club collection, they conferred full intellectual property rights for that Ape to whomever owns it. This is an uncommon move, but it's worth considering for anyone creating an NFT collection as a potential aspect to make each NFT more valuable.

Unfortunately, many variables are limited by a simple constraint: file size.

File Size

The issue of file size is a significant concern when it comes to NFTs, particularly with regard to storing and transferring them on the blockchain. Because NFTs are typically comprised of digital files, such as images or videos, the size of these files can be quite large, particularly for high-quality or high-resolution content. This presents a challenge for blockchain networks, which have limited storage capacity and bandwidth.

One approach to addressing this issue is to use compression techniques to reduce the size of the files without sacrificing quality. However, there is a trade-off between file size and quality, and in some cases, compression can lead to loss of detail or visual artifacts that can negatively impact the value of an NFT.

The most common approach is to store files off-chain, rather than on the blockchain itself. This involves storing the file on a separate server or cloud storage platform and linking to it from the NFT using a unique identifier or hash value. This approach can help reduce the size of the NFT on the blockchain while still providing access to the original file when needed. However, it also introduces additional complexity and potential points of failure – the off-chain storage platform must be maintained and accessible in order to access the file.

This approach has also been a point of controversy in the NFT community, with some accusing it of being a scam.

Off-chain storage requires that the unique identifier or hash value used to link to the file be kept secure and accessible, which can be a challenge in itself. Also, keeping the storage platform online can be problematic if the platform goes down or is hacked, which can compromise the authenticity of the NFT.

This also creates a vulnerability where the person who created the NFT and the off-chain storage can modify the file stored off-chain, effectively destroying the NFT from afar. This vulnerability was demonstrated in 2021 by the founder of encrypted messaging app Signal, who sold NFTs that pointed to a file he later replaced with a poop emoji to serve as a cautionary tale.

Storage Considerations

To address these concerns, some NFT creators have turned to decentralized storage solutions such as IPFS (InterPlanetary File System) or Arweave. These platforms offer a more secure and decentralized approach to file storage, which can help to mitigate the potential risks associated with off-chain storage. These solutions are not perfect, but continue to improve over time.

Despite these concerns, off-chain storage remains a popular approach for many NFT creators, as it allows them to create and sell NFTs without having to worry about the limitations of on-chain storage. However, NFT buyers should understand the associated risks and carefully evaluate the authenticity and value of the NFT before making a purchase.

The BSV (Bitcoin Satoshi Vision) blockchain, which is a fork of the original Bitcoin blockchain, has taken a different approach to the NFT file size issue. Unlike other blockchains, which limit the size of individual transactions, the BSV blockchain allows for much larger transactions as it has no cap on the block size. This is because the BSV blockchain is focused on enabling large-scale data applications.

By allowing for larger transactions, the BSV blockchain is able to store more information on-chain, including larger NFT files. This approach eliminates the need for off-chain storage. Additionally, it can reduce the transaction costs associated with creating and transferring NFTs, as larger transactions on other blockchains can be more expensive.

However, the larger transaction size limit of the BSV blockchain also introduces potential security risks. Large transactions can take longer to propagate through the network and be validated by nodes, potentially leaving them vulnerable to attack. Additionally, larger transactions can also be used to bloat the blockchain and consume more storage and processing resources.

File size presents a significant challenge for NFT creators and collectors, particularly as the demand for high-quality and high-resolution content continues to grow. Finding a balance between file size, quality, and accessibility is critical to ensure the long-term value and viability of NFTs as a digital asset class.

Ultimately, the aspects or variables of an NFT will depend on the specific use case and the intended market. For example, a collectible card might have different intrinsic and extrinsic variables than a piece of virtual real estate. It is important to carefully consider the aspects and variables of an NFT to create a unique and valuable digital asset.

Content and Chain Selection

Once you have determined the aspects of your NFT, the next step is to create the digital content that will make up the NFT. This could include creating the artwork or other digital media, or it could involve compiling and organizing existing content into a format that can be tokenized as an NFT. Make sure the digital content is of high quality and properly licensed, or at least attributed to the appropriate creators.

Once the digital file for the NFT is created, the next step is to prepare the metadata. This includes information such as the name of the NFT, a description of the artwork, and the artist's name. Additionally, metadata can include any additional attributes that are relevant to the NFT, such as its rarity or edition number.

This information is stored on the blockchain along with the digital file, creating a permanent record of the NFT's characteristics. It is also used to provide information about the NFT's provenance, ownership, and other relevant details. The metadata should be carefully curated and should accurately reflect the unique qualities and characteristics of the NFT.

Once you have created the digital content and metadata for your NFT, the next step is to choose the blockchain on which you will mint the NFT.

This typically involves choosing a chain that supports NFTs and selecting a compatible smart contract to use for minting the NFT. Ensure the blockchain and smart contract you choose are secure and well maintained, as this helps maintain the long-term viability and value of your NFT.

Ethereum is currently the most widely used blockchain for creating and trading NFTs. The ERC-721 and ERC-1155 smart contracts are specifically designed for creating and managing NFTs. They are supported by a wide range of wallets, marketplaces, and other NFT-related tools. These contracts have been used to create NFTs for a wide range of use cases, including art, music, gaming, and collectibles.

For art, music, and collectibles, the ERC-721 contract is a popular choice, as it allows for the creation of unique, one-of-a-kind NFTs that can be used to represent individual pieces of content. For gaming and other use cases that involve the creation of multiple, identical NFTs, the ERC-1155 contract is often used, as it allows for the creation of semi-fungible NFTs sometimes called SFTs that can be used to represent multiple copies of the same content.

In addition to Ethereum, other blockchains are also being used to create and trade NFTs. For example, the Binance Smart Chain (BSC) and Polygon networks have gained popularity as alternatives to Ethereum due to their lower transaction fees and faster transaction times. The Binance Smart Chain supports the creation of NFTs using the BEP-721 and BEP-1155 smart contracts, while Polygon still uses the ERC-1155 and ERC-721 contracts.

Other blockchains that support NFTs include the Flow blockchain, which is specifically designed for creating NFTs and other digital assets for use in games and other applications, and the Tezos blockchain, which supports NFTs through the FA2 token standard. The Polkadot blockchain also supports NFTs through the Substrate framework, which allows for the creation of custom smart contracts.

When it comes to specific use cases, there are certain blockchains and smart contracts that may be more optimal. For example, the WAX blockchain has gained popularity in the collectibles space, due to its focus on creating a user-friendly experience for creating and trading NFTs. The WAX blockchain uses the AtomicAssets standard, which is specifically designed for creating NFTs for use in games, collectibles, and other applications.

In the music industry, there are several platforms that have emerged to help artists create and sell NFTs. These include platforms such as Audius, which uses the Solana blockchain, and Royal, which uses the Ethereum blockchain. These platforms are specifically designed to help musicians create and sell NFTs that represent their music, and often include features such as royalty tracking and revenue sharing.

In the event ticketing space, blockchains such as the Hedera Hashgraph and the Polygon network are being used to create NFT-based ticketing systems. These systems allow event organizers to create NFTs that represent tickets to their events, which can then be securely transferred and verified using the blockchain. This helps to reduce fraud and ensure that only legitimate ticket holders are able to attend the event.

Finally, you will need to choose a marketplace on which to list and sell your NFT.

There are a number of popular NFT marketplaces, such as OpenSea, Rarible, and SuperRare, each of which has its own strengths and weaknesses. Choose a marketplace that is well suited to the particular qualities and characteristics of your NFT and that has a strong user base.

Wallets

Cryptocurrency wallets are a crucial component of the NFT ecosystem, as they are used to store, manage, and transfer NFTs. You will need to have a cryptocurrency wallet that supports the chain on which you plan to mint and trade your NFTs.

There are many different types of cryptocurrency wallets available, including desktop wallets, mobile wallets, and hardware wallets. Desktop wallets are software programs that you install on your computer. They are convenient for users who want to store their NFTs on their computer and have easy access to them. One of the benefits of desktop wallets is that they are typically free to use and offer a high degree of security if properly configured.

Desktop wallets do have vulnerability to malware and hacking attempts, which could result in the loss of your NFTs. Also, if your computer crashes or is stolen, you could lose access to your NFTs.

Mobile wallets are apps that you download to your smartphone or tablet. They are convenient for users who want to access their NFTs on the go. One of the benefits of mobile wallets is that they are typically easy to use and offer a high degree of accessibility.

However, mobile wallets may not offer the same level of security as desktop or hardware wallets. Unfortunately, if you lose your phone or it is stolen, you could lose access to your NFTs unless you have a backup of your wallet.

Hardware wallets are physical devices that you connect to your computer or smartphone. They are convenient for users who want to safeguard their NFTs with air-gapped storage to protect them from hacking attempts and malware. Hardware wallets are typically considered the most secure option digital assets like NFTs; they offer an extra layer of security through the use of a physical device.

One drawback to hardware wallets is that they can be expensive to purchase, and may require some technical knowledge to set up and use properly. In addition, hardware wallets can be damaged or stolen, which could cause irreparable loss.

Regardless of the type of wallet you choose, it is imperative that you back it up and follow best practices for wallet security. This includes creating a strong, unique password, enabling two-factor authentication, and transcribing up your wallet's seed phrase or private key then storing it in a secure location.

Since wallets are very commonly secured with a 12- or 24-word mnemonic seed phrase, those who create them must write this seed phrase down in a secure location should something happens to their wallet, and make certain never to show this phrase to anyone or risk it in any way. Do not allow it to be seen by any cameras, and do not read it out loud.

Additionally, it is important to only download wallets and other cryptocurrency-related software from trusted sources and to be vigilant for phishing scams and other forms of fraud that could compromise your wallet's security.

Consider factors such as security, ease of use, and compatibility with the chain you plan to use when choosing a wallet. Some wallets are designed specifically for certain chains, while others support many. Choose a wallet that allows you to maintain control over your private keys.

One of the most popular options for storing and managing NFTs is the MetaMask wallet. MetaMask is a browser extension that is free to use and is available for Chrome, Firefox, Brave, and other popular browsers. There is also a mobile app available for Android and iOS devices. It allows users to connect to decentralized applications (dApps) on various blockchains, including Ethereum and Polygon, and is compatible with a wide range of NFT marketplaces and platforms.

Another popular option is the Trust Wallet, which is a mobile wallet that supports a variety of blockchains. Trust Wallet is commonly praised its ease of use and intuitive interface.

When it comes to hardware wallets, some of the most popular options are the Ledger Nano or Trezor. While they often operate in a stand-alone environment and are mainly suited for providing an offline, cold storage solution for storing cryptocurrency and NFTs rather than facilitating active usage, there have been advances on this front.

Trezor, for example, has an integration with the popular software wallet Exodus which makes using your NFTs easier. Also, while Ledgers were long considered the gold standard for hardware wallets, their controversial move to offer "seed phrase recovery" services has called their security into question.

To create a MetaMask wallet, the first thing to do is go to the MetaMask website and click "Get Extension", selecting the relevant choice based on your browser. Install the extension and follow the prompts to create a new wallet. Write down your seed phrase and store it somewhere safe. You can then connect it to various dApps that support NFT transactions by clicking the MetaMask extension.

As for the Trust Wallet, download the app from the App Store or Google Play Store then open it. Write down your seed phrase and store it somewhere safe. At that point the wallet is set up, and you can connect it to various dApps that support NFT transactions by using the built-in web browser.

After all this is done, you can start interacting with NFTs. If you want to buy or sell an NFT, connect your wallet to a marketplace and authorize transactions through your wallet. The process may differ slightly depending on the specific dApp and transaction, but generally involves following a few prompts within the wallet app to confirm the transaction and pay any associated fees.

Nearly every activity on a blockchain requires the user to pay a transaction fee. Transaction fees, or gas fees, are part of almost every blockchain. Any transaction on a blockchain network carries a fee paid to the network to compensate the nodes for processing the transaction. Fees tend to be paid in the chain's native cryptocurrency.

The size of the fee depends on several factors, such as the network's congestion, the complexity of the transaction, the desired processing time, and some intrinsic aspects of the blockchain in question such as its consensus mechanism. The more congested the network is, the higher the fees. Miners and validators prioritize transactions with higher fees since they earn more rewards for processing them.

Purchase the needed assets on exchanges or get them from other users. Remember to monitor transaction fees regularly to avoid paying excessive amounts for transactions.

Marketplaces

Once a user has a cryptocurrency wallet and obtained the required assets to pay transaction fees, the next step to participating in the NFT ecosystem is to obtain the NFTs themselves. Many projects have their own proprietary NFT marketplaces where you can buy assets specific to their ecosystem, but there are also several popular marketplaces that sell nearly any NFT on the blockchains they support.

OpenSea is a popular and user-friendly NFT marketplace that allows users to buy, sell, and discover NFTs. To create an account on OpenSea, simply visit the website and click the "Sign Up" button in the top-right corner of the home page. You will then be prompted to create an account using your email address, Google, or Apple account. Once you have created your account, you can start browsing NFTs, creating collections, and interacting with other users on the platform.

When creating an account on OpenSea, it is important to keep in mind that you will need to link a cryptocurrency wallet to your account in order to buy, sell, or create NFTs. OpenSea supports a variety of different wallets, including MetaMask, WalletConnect, and Coinbase Wallet. To link your wallet to your OpenSea account, simply go to your account settings and select "Wallets" from the drop-down menu. You will then be prompted to connect your wallet by entering your wallet address or scanning a QR code.

Once your wallet is linked to your OpenSea account, you can start buying, selling, and creating NFTs.

Buying and Selling Basics

Buying an NFT is relatively simple.

Browse the marketplace and find an NFT that you like. You can then place a bid or buy it outright using cryptocurrency. OpenSea primarily operates on the Ethereum blockchain, which means that users typically need to have Ethereum or another cryptocurrency in order to buy an

NFT. However, OpenSea has partnered with MoonPay to enable purchases with credit cards in some cases, making it possible to use fiat currency to purchase certain NFTs on OpenSea through a feature called "Instant Buy."

Instant Buy allows users to purchase NFTs using a card, which is then converted to Ethereum by the third-party payment processor. This allows users who do not have cryptocurrency to buy NFTs using traditional payment methods.

To use Instant Buy on OpenSea, users must first connect their credit card or debit card to their OpenSea account. This is done by navigating to the "Instant Buy" tab on the OpenSea home page and following the prompts to enter payment information.

Once a payment method is added, users can search for NFTs that are available for purchase using Instant Buy. These NFTs will have an "Instant Buy" button next to them on the OpenSea marketplace. Clicking this button will initiate the purchase process and allow users to buy the NFT using their connected payment method.

Not all NFTs on OpenSea are available for purchase using Instant Buy. This feature is only available for certain NFTs that have been approved by OpenSea's team. Additionally, Instant Buy purchases are subject to a fee of 2.5% of the purchase price. Selling an NFT is more complex.

You will need to create a listing for it on the marketplace, including details such as the price, description, and any relevant metadata. You must also create the NFT itself in advance, keeping in mind all the aspects and variables you care to integrate as you do so. Once your NFT is listed, other users can make offers or buy it outright via the process outlined earlier.

Selecting a Marketplace

As mentioned earlier, there are many NFT marketplaces that users can consider, each with their own unique features and user experiences. One such platform is SuperRare, which is known for its curated selection of high-quality NFTs and its emphasis on supporting artists.

To create an account on SuperRare, users must first apply for approval through a verification process that involves submitting samples of their artwork and personal information. Once approved, users can create a profile and start browsing and bidding on NFTs.

Another popular NFT marketplace is Nifty Gateway, which is known for its high-profile artist collaborations and limited-edition drops. To create an account on Nifty Gateway, users can simply sign up with their email address and link a payment method, such as a credit card or bank account.

Finally, Rarible is another NFT marketplace that is popular among independent artists and creators. Unlike SuperRare and Nifty Gateway, Rarible allows users to create and sell their own NFTs without the need for a third-party verification process. To create an account on Rarible, users can simply sign up with an email address and connect their cryptocurrency wallet.

These are only a few of the many marketplaces which offer support for a wide variety of NFTs. More are provided in the appendices to this book. Explore multiple platforms and understand the different options and user experiences they offer to find the best platform for you.

Many niche marketplaces that cater to specific ecosystems or use cases also exist.

One example is the Axie Infinity Marketplace, which is specifically designed for buying and selling Axie NFTs for use in games created by Axie Infinity publisher Sky Mavis. Axies are creatures that players can use to battle and earn rewards within the Axie Infinity universe. NFTs are used to represent ownership of these creatures.

To participate in the Axie Infinity Marketplace, users must first create an account on the Axie Infinity platform. The user can then acquire Axies by buying them on the marketplace, earning them through gameplay, or participating in a scholarship program. Once they have acquired Axies, they can then list them for sale on the Axie Infinity Marketplace or purchase other Axies listed by other players, although scholars are not permitted to sell their Axies as they do not own them but are merely borrowing them.

Transaction Details

The Axie Infinity Marketplace uses a Dutch auction format, where the price of the NFT is gradually lowered until a buyer is found. NFT marketplaces can use a variety of other auction formats, each with their own advantages and disadvantages.

An English Auction is the most common type of auction used in NFT marketplaces. These auctions start with a low price and gradually increase until a buyer is found. Bidders place bids that are higher than the current bid, and the highest bidder at the end of the auction wins the item.

In a Vickrey auction, bidders submit sealed bids, and the highest bidder wins the item at the second-highest bid price. This type of auction is used to encourage bidders to submit their true valuations of an item, as there is no incentive to bid lower than what they believe the item is worth.

A sealed bid auction is where bidders submit their bids in a sealed "envelope," and the highest bidder wins the item at their bid price. This type of auction is commonly used in art auctions and can help to keep bids private and prevent auction sniping.

Hybrid auctions combine two or more types of auctions to create a unique bidding process. For example, an auction might start with a Dutch auction format and then switch to a Vickrey auction once the price has reached a certain level. This can help to balance the advantages and disadvantages of each type of auction and create a more dynamic bidding process.

The type of auctions a marketplace supports is one of many considerations to account for when deciding whether to create an account on any given NFT marketplace. However, there are other factors to consider besides the platform's ease of use and user interface.

One should always consider the blockchain(s) a marketplace supports. This determines the types of NFTs that can be traded on the platform. Some marketplaces may only support NFTs minted on Ethereum, while others may support a variety of blockchains such as Binance Smart Chain, Polygon, or Flow.

Another factor is the fees charged. This can include fees for listing NFTs for sale, transaction fees for buying or selling NFTs, and royalties paid to the original creator of the NFT. Research and compare the fees charged by different marketplaces to find the one that offers the best value for your needs.

Whether the marketplace supports royalty payments to the original creators of NFTs is important. Many artists and creators rely on royalties as a source of income. Some marketplaces, such as Foundation, prioritize supporting artists and enforce royalties on secondary sales of the NFTs to continue supporting creators. Other marketplaces may not incorporate this requirement and it is important account for that.

Additionally, users should consider the market share and availability of NFTs on each marketplace. Some NFT marketplaces have a larger user base and a wider selection of NFTs, while others are more niche and offer a more limited selection of NFTs. It may be beneficial to research the popularity and reputation of each marketplace before choosing where to buy or sell NFTs.

It is important to carefully research and consider different NFT marketplaces before creating an account or buying/selling NFTs. By understanding the features and limitations of each marketplace, users can make informed decisions that maximize the potential for success and profitability in the NFT space.

Finally, it may be worth considering the reputation and community surrounding each NFT marketplace. This can include factors such as the marketplace's history of security and transparency as well as the level of activity and innovation within the platform. Considering these factors allows users to make informed decisions about which NFT marketplaces to join and which ones are best suited to their needs and interests.

Selling

Once you have settled on a marketplace, the next step for a seller is creating a collection. For a buyer, you are largely browsing NFTs listed as part of collections when deciding what to purchase based on your motivations. Sellers must create these collections.

Creating an NFT collection allows you to group together a set of NFTs that share a common theme, such as a collection of artwork or a set of trading cards. This can make it easier for buyers to find and purchase your NFTs and can also increase their value by creating a sense of exclusivity and rarity.

Most major NFT marketplaces, such as OpenSea, Rarible, and Nifty Gateway, support collections. Niche ones may not support them, or may have NFTs grouped into specific collections which already exist in ways that are hard-coded by the developers based on the NFTs attributes.

Once you've chosen a marketplace, created an account, and verified your identity (if applicable), you'll need to decide on the theme and design of your NFT collection. This depends on the attributes and variables of your NFTs which you decided upon earlier if you are creating your own NFTs, or curating a set of existing assets that fit the theme of your collection. Consider the market demand for your chosen theme, as well as the quality and uniqueness of your assets, to maximize the value of your NFTs.

Once you've decided on your theme and assets, you can begin the process of creating your NFT collection on the marketplace.

In the case of a general NFT marketplace, you will typically be prompted to enter a name and description for your collection. This helps buyers understand what your collection is about and what they can expect from it. Then you will need to upload the metadata and digital assets for each NFT in the collection. This typically involves uploading an image or video file, along with any additional information about the NFT such as its name, description, and attributes. After that, specify any royalty or commission percentages that you wish to receive when your NFTs are resold.

Finally, review and confirm the details of your NFT collection before it is listed for sale. This may involve reviewing the marketplace's terms and conditions, but generally involves setting prices and other details for your NFTs.

Once your NFT collection is live on the marketplace, you can start promoting it to potential buyers and tracking its performance over time. This involves sharing it on social media or other online platforms, participating in NFT communities and forums, and reaching out to collectors or influencers in your niche. Building awareness and interest in your collection increases the likelihood of sales and maximize the value of your NFTs.

Take note: in most cases, this is a months-long process which is usually started well in advance of creating your NFTs. The moment a prospective NFT seller has the idea to create and sell a collection is when they should ideally begin building a community and interest. This way, prospective buyers are already waiting for these NFTs well before they are minted or sold.

If you already have an NFT that you have uploaded, this is where the process typically ends. However, if you are creating new NFTs, they still need to be minted. Most marketplaces recommend that you do not mint your NFTs until they sell to save on transaction fees, so this is often the last step in the life cycle of an NFT transaction on a marketplace.

Without minting the NFT, it doesn't actually exist except as a concept in the mind of its creator.

Minting and Whitelisting

To mint an NFT, one typically interacts with the smart contract via a dApp using a Web3-enabled wallet, which enables them to send transactions to the blockchain. They must have enough gas to pay the fees.

Once the transaction is sent, it will be processed by the network and included in the next block. This process typically takes a few seconds to a few minutes, depending on the blockchain and the current network congestion. Once the transaction is confirmed, the NFT will be minted. Depending on the dApp used to interact with the smart contract, the NFT may be sent to the creator's wallet or to some other wallet address.

Many NFT creators sell them through a process called "whitelisting," where rather than minting the NFTs directly, they "whitelist" community members who do the minting themselves. Oftentimes creators sell these whitelist spots or give them to highly engaged community members as rewards for driving greater interest in their collection. This enables some community members to buy NFTs from the collection at an initial starting price.

This is generally a more complex process, but helps ensure buyers exist before the collection is listed for sale. Some creators though prefer to list directly on marketplaces and use the marketplace to mint NFTs.

OpenSea's dApp can provide an example of how this works. To mint an NFT using OpenSea's interface, create a new item and upload the digital asset and metadata for the NFT. Users also set a price and royalty percentage here.

Select the "Create" option and choose the smart contract they want to use to mint the NFT. OpenSea supports a range of smart contracts for NFTs, including the popular ERC-721 and ERC-1155 standards. Then sign and send the transaction to the blockchain, which contains the data needed to create the NFT.

Recall that "signing" a transaction uses the digital signature associated with the user's cryptocurrency wallet to verify the authenticity of the proposed activity. In some cases, a simple signature can be done without a gas fee, but when creating an NFT, the user is also sending a transaction, which requires a fee.

If a user opts to have OpenSea only mint an NFT upon sale, rather than in advance, this means that the NFT will not be created until a buyer purchases it. In this case, users need not pay the transaction fee for minting the NFT upfront, as it will be paid by the buyer as part of the purchase transaction. This can be a useful option for creators who do not want to pay upfront, or who are uncertain whether there is sufficient demand for their NFT to justify the cost of minting it in advance.

Once minted, the NFT appears in the user's connected wallet as a new token with a unique identifier. The user can then list the NFT for sale on a marketplace, transfer it to another wallet, or use it in any manner they wish. Any transactions using the NFT will incur another fee, and possibly charge a royalty.

Summary

Choosing the right NFT marketplace is one of the foundational steps for sellers. Renowned platforms like OpenSea, Rarible, and Nifty Gateway are often preferred, although some niche platforms present unique attributes, sometimes even offering hard-coded collections. Collections are an integral part of NFT marketplaces, so organizing NFTs by shared themes is an important consideration.

Defining a collection requires creators to select the theme and design of their NFTs with care. While this might simply be a curation of existing assets, a collection more frequently reflects the innate attributes of the NFTs a creator intends to sell.

The next stage is the listing process, where sellers market their collections with labels and descriptions. This process helps the targeted buyers identify that this collection is suitable for them. Subsequent steps involve the uploading of metadata, digital assets, and the specifics of royalties or commission percentages for potential resale. Before any collection launches on the marketplace, sellers would do well to reviewing details all the details, including pricing, of their assets and ensure everything aligns with their objectives.

Successful NFT sales frequently owe their results to marketing and promotional strategies every bit as much as the details and value of the NFTs themselves. Sellers are advised to cultivate anticipation and demand long before the NFTs are minted – engaging potential buyers through social media channels, vibrant forums, and interactions with esteemed collectors is a crucial part of this process.

Minting, the point where an NFT is actually created on the blockchain, is often best delayed as long as possible to minimize unnecessary expenses. In many cases this is one of the last steps in the process of creating and selling an NFT for the first time. In other situations, minting occurred long before the transaction and the asset is now just changing hands. The process of whitelisting enables community members to mint the NFT directly rather than the seller themselves, possibly giving them a certain level of control over what they receive or possibly leaving it entirely up to chance. Either way, this allows the actual creator to save on fees.

From start to finish using OpenSea as an example, creators start by uploading the digital asset and metadata, determine the price, and decide on any royalties. The next step involves choosing a smart contract, signing, and sending the transaction to the chosen blockchain. Choosing to only mint when a sale is made allows the creator sidesteps the initial fees, with the buyer shouldering. The NFT is then sent to the purchaser's wallet with its unique ID. At this point, many may simply attempt to flip the NFT for a profit, but for assets with real utility, this is a much less frequent occurrence. NFTs that truly serve some purpose apart from enriching the creator through sales are retained longer and employed by their owners to further their desires.

CHAPTER 4

NFT Disruption and Innovation in the Art World

The art world has long been a space for creative expression and cultural significance, with physical works of art being bought, sold, and collected by enthusiasts for centuries. However, the digital age has also brought about transformative changes with one of the most significant being the emergence of NFTs. This chapter delves into the adoption of NFTs in the art world, the benefits for artists and collectors, and the controversies that have arisen as a result, and offers a comprehensive strategy for those looking to successfully implement NFTs into their artistic endeavors.

The Rise of NFTs in the Art World

For centuries, a creator and collector of physical art would display their art in a physical space, like a museum or even in their own living rooms. Ownership and authenticity of that art was also easy to prove as collectors could certify their authenticity through independent experts and from the artist themselves. The key difference between physical art and digital art is that the latter is digital and exists in a virtual form. Digital art can include illustrations, photographs, GIFs, 3D models, and more. However, digital art can easily be copied and displayed. For instance, if we see a picture we like on the Web, we can simply screenshot the digital art, or in many cases just save the image as a PDF or JPEG on our own computers, to be displayed wherever and whenever we want.

NFTs are used for digital art because they can certify the authenticity of the artwork and provide a permanent record of ownership. By tokenizing the artwork and recording it on the blockchain, buyers of the artwork can have confidence that it is the original work.

Additionally, NFTs can be used to create scarcity for digital art, making it a valuable asset. This is why digital art is one of the earliest implementations of NFTs ushering in the implementation of the renaissance of blockchain in the art world. In other words, an NFT functions as a digital certificate of ownership for a given asset and is distinct from any other NFT in circulation. Because of this feature, NFTs are being used to certify ownership of digital art.

This technology also facilitates the buying and selling of NFTs as well as the storage of ownership information on the blockchain, allowing for the digital asset to be exchanged, tracked, and managed on the blockchain.

Early NFT Art Projects and Impact on the Art World

The application of NFTs has brought about significant changes in the art world, offering new possibilities for creative expression, ownership, and trading. Some of the earliest implementations of NFTs in the art world were projects such as CryptoPunks and CryptoKitties, paving the way for numerous artists and collectors to explore this new frontier.

CryptoPunks, created by software developers Matt Hall and John Watkinson of Larva Labs, debuted in June 2017 as one of the earliest examples of NFT art projects. The project consists of 10,000 unique 24x24 pixel art characters, with each Punk featuring a distinct combination of attributes, such as different hairstyles, facial expressions, and accessories. Originally, these digital characters were available for free to anyone with an Ethereum wallet. However, as demand grew, the value of these Punks rapidly increased, with some selling for hundreds of thousands or even millions of dollars.

CryptoPunks' success signaled the potential of NFTs as a medium for digital art and collectibles. The project demonstrated that unique digital items could hold value and be traded on blockchain platforms like Ethereum. In addition, it showcased the significance of provable scarcity and ownership in the digital art world, as the immutable nature of blockchain technology ensured that each Punk could not be replicated or counterfeited since each Punk has a different value based on when the art was minted.

In November 2017, a new implementation of digital art called CryptoKitties showed the art world how gaming and art could converge. CryptoKitties, developed by Axiom Zen (now Dapper Labs), was a virtual breeding game built also on the Ethereum network. Users could collect, breed, and trade digital cats, each with its distinct genetic traits that could be passed down to their offspring. The project gained widespread popularity. At its peak, the game even accounted for a significant percentage of transactions on the Ethereum network, even causing slowdowns on the network. (These problems exposed potential scalability issues of blockchain platforms at that time.)

As the success of CryptoPunks and CryptoKitties reverberated throughout the art world, artists began to experiment with digital art forms, exploring the possibilities that this new medium offered. Meanwhile, social media and online platforms emerged as bustling marketplaces where artists could showcase their works and collectors could seek out new and exciting pieces. In the past, an art object would often take years and sometimes centuries to gain the attention of the masses. With these new social networks and digital bazaars, an artist could quickly draw attention to their creation in days, if not a few hours. It was in these digital bazaars that artists began to see the true potential of NFTs.

One of these artists was Mike Winkelmann, also known as "Beeple." "Everydays: The First 5000 Days" is a collection of 5,000 images created by Beeple over a 13-year period which were then compiled into a single, collective piece. The artwork was sold as an NFT. The sale of "Everydays: The First 5000 Days" was a landmark event in the history of digital art as it was the first NFT artwork to sell at a major auction house. Sold for over $65 million, it set the record for the most money spent on digital art. This sale has had a major impact on the art world as it has given digital art, and NFTs in particular, the legitimacy that it lacked.

Other high-profile NFT sales have since followed, including the sale of Grimes' "WarNymph" for over $6 million and the sale of "Crossroads 2" by artist Pak for over $16 million. These auctions have had a major impact on the art world and are sure to shape the future of digital art for years to come.

The Adoption of NFTs by Established Artists and Brands

The legitimization of NFTs in the digital art brought on by Beeple's and other successes has paved the way for established artists and brands to monetize their artwork and merchandise.

Established brands and companies have released limited-edition and exclusive products as NFTs. For example, the NBA recently released a series of NFT trading cards, called The Association, where the collectible's design changes over time. The appearance of the NFTs evolves based on players' on-court performance. The more accomplished a player is throughout the season, the more their NFT will visually change. Besides this NFT initiative, the NBA has heavily contributed to putting sports NFTs on the map through Dapper Labs' NBA Top Shot. In 2022, the platform was largely responsible for the NFT sports-craze driving sales that reached almost $1 billion.

In addition to monetization, established artists and brands have also adopted NFTs to increase engagement with their fans, customers, and followers. For example, music artist Steve Aoki recently released an NFT collection that includes limited-edition digital art pieces and merchandise. Other artists and brands have leveraged NFTs for marketing campaigns, offering rewards to fans who purchase their NFTs.

The Benefits of NFTs for Artists and Collectors

Overall, the use of NFTs by established artists and brands is proving to be beneficial. NFTs offer a way for artists to monetize and certify their artwork, and for brands to create exclusive products and incentive-based marketing campaigns. The use of NFTs by these established entities is making digital art and collectibles more widely accepted.

Financial Benefits

The examples of Beeple's and Steve Aoki's NFT collections have illustrated the potential financial benefits to artists and collectors by selling original creations. But aside from the sale of these NFT collections, there are further opportunities to earn royalties through platforms that offer "secondary sales royalties" features. By using these features, the artist can set a certain percentage of the purchase price of the secondary sale to be paid to them as royalty. For example, the artist might set a 5% royalty on secondary sales, so they will receive 5% from the purchase price of any secondary sales of their NFTs. In addition to setting a percentage on secondary sales royalties, the artist can also designate different license types on the platform. This allows the artist to control how their artwork is used, giving them more control over their creative work in addition to creating additional royalty streams.

There are a number of platforms available for artists that feature secondary sales royalty options. Some popular examples include SuperRare, MakersPlace, Foundation, and OpenSea, among others. Each of these platforms offers different features and services, so be sure to do your own research to find the best one for you.

In addition to these platforms, there are also a number of blockchain-based projects that are specifically tailored toward artists. These projects often feature various tools to help artists monetize and protect their artwork, such as royalty payment services and copyright management.

Finally, there are also traditional platforms that are beginning to offer NFTs and secondary sales royalty features. Platforms such as eBay and Patreon are two examples of this, and more platforms are sure to follow.

Provenance and Authentication

Provenance and authentication are two critical components of the art world. Provenance refers to the history of ownership of a piece of art, while authentication is the process of verifying that a piece of art is genuine. Both of these factors can significantly impact the value of an artwork, making them essential for artists looking to sell their work.

Recently, NFTs have emerged as a new tool for artists to benefit from provenance and authentication. NFTs are unique digital tokens that are used to represent ownership of a digital asset, such as a piece of art. When an artist creates an NFT for their work, they can include information about the artwork's provenance, such as its previous owners and exhibition history.

By including this information, artists can increase the value of their work by providing potential buyers with a sense of the artwork's history and significance. This can help to establish the artwork's authenticity and validate its value. Additionally, the use of NFTs can provide artists with a greater degree of control over the distribution and ownership of their work, allowing them to maintain ownership and potentially receive royalties each time their work is sold.

The use of NFTs can also help to protect artists from fraud and theft. As NFTs are stored on a blockchain, they are virtually impossible to counterfeit or manipulate. This makes it much more difficult for fraudsters to pass off fake artwork as genuine, helping to protect both artists and buyers.

Expanding Opportunities for Emerging Artists Through Democratization

The democratization of the art market is having a major impact on the opportunity for emerging artists largely due to NFTs. The traditional art market is often seen as closed off and inaccessible to emerging artists, with galleries and other outlets often having high requirements for entry. However, with democratization, more and more artists are finding opportunities to showcase their work without the need for an institutional setting. By tokenizing artwork and recording it on the blockchain, artists can have confidence that their work will be protected and its authenticity certified. This allows the artist to create a digital marketplace for their work, giving them more control and creating more opportunities for them to reach a wider audience.

Additionally, the use of digital platforms has also contributed to the democratization of the art market. Platforms such as Instagram, Twitter, and YouTube allow artists to share their work and connect with potential buyers. These platforms also allow for more interaction between the artist and the audience, allowing for meaningful engagement and feedback.

The Appeal of Digital Art for Collectors

Thanks to the emergence of digital ownership and the increasing appeal of unique, one-of-a-kind items, NFTs have also transformed the market for collectors. With NFTs, collectors now have the opportunity to own digital assets that are unique, rare, and verifiably authentic, opening up a whole new world of investment opportunities.

One of the key appeals of digital ownership for collectors is the sense of exclusivity and uniqueness that comes with owning a one-of-a-kind item. With traditional collectibles such as art or sports memorabilia, there may be multiple copies of the same item, leading to a dilution of value. With NFTs, however, each item is unique, with its own distinct properties and attributes, ensuring that its value remains high.

The emergence of NFTs has also created new investment opportunities for collectors. With traditional collectibles, the value of an item is often tied to the broader market for that particular type of item. With NFTs, however, the value is determined solely by supply and demand, creating the potential for significant returns on investment.

Moreover, NFTs are highly portable, meaning that they can be easily bought and sold on digital marketplaces, offering collectors greater liquidity and flexibility in their investments. This has led to the creation of a whole new ecosystem of digital marketplaces and platforms, catering specifically to the trading of NFTs.

Controversies Surrounding NFTs in the Art World

The emergence of NFTs has revolutionized the art world, providing new opportunities for artists and collectors alike. However, NFTs have sparked heated debates within the art community.

Environmental Concerns

One of the most prominent controversies surrounding NFTs is their impact on the environment. The creation and trading of NFTs on blockchain networks like Ethereum require significant computational power, resulting in high energy consumption and, consequently, a substantial carbon footprint. Critics argue that the art world's embrace of NFTs is contributing to climate change, undermining efforts to reduce carbon emissions and promote sustainability.

On the other hand, proponents of NFTs point out that many blockchain networks are transitioning to more energy-efficient consensus mechanisms, such as Ethereum's shift from proof of work to proof of stake. Additionally, some NFT platforms are adopting eco-friendly practices, like carbon offsetting, to mitigate their environmental impact.

Artistic Integrity and Authenticity

Another controversy is the debate surrounding artistic integrity and authenticity. Some critics argue that the digital nature of NFTs makes it easier for artists to plagiarize or misrepresent other creators' works. They contend that the absence of a physical artifact reduces the perceived value of digital art and fosters an environment where intellectual property rights may be disregarded.

In contrast, NFT supporters assert that blockchain technology can actually enhance the authenticity and provenance of digital art. Through the decentralized ledger, the ownership and transfer history of an NFT can be securely tracked and verified, making it difficult for forgeries to enter the market. They argue that NFTs provide an opportunity for artists to protect their work in the digital realm, where plagiarism has long been a pervasive issue.

Commodification of Art and Culture

Critics argue that the rise of NFTs has led to the over-commercialization of art, with collectors and speculators treating digital artworks more like tradable assets than meaningful creative expressions. This shift, they claim, could lead to a focus on financial gain at the expense of artistic merit and cultural significance.

However, NFT proponents argue that the art world has always been intertwined with commerce, and NFTs are simply a new medium for artists to monetize their work. They maintain that the financial success of NFTs can enable artists to sustain themselves and fund future projects, ultimately enriching the cultural landscape.

Exclusivity and Accessibility

Lastly, the issues of exclusivity and accessibility have been key points of contention in the NFT art world. Some argue that NFTs perpetuate the art world's elitist nature by catering to wealthy collectors and creating a barrier to entry for those with fewer financial resources. They contend that this could lead to the further marginalization of underrepresented artists and communities.

On the other hand, supporters highlight the role of NFTs in democratizing the art market. They assert that NFT platforms provide emerging artists with the opportunity to showcase their work to a global audience, bypassing traditional gatekeepers like galleries and auction houses. Additionally, fractional ownership of NFTs has been proposed to increase accessibility to digital art for a wider range of collectors.

Strategies for Artists and Collectors

The digital art world has experienced a transformative shift with the emergence of NFTs, presenting new opportunities for artists and collectors alike. As more individuals enter the NFT art market, it is essential to understand the strategies that can help them succeed in this rapidly evolving landscape.

Here are some key strategies that both artists and collectors should consider when entering the NFT art world.

I. Strategies for Artists

   A. Establish a Unique Artistic Identity

      1. Develop a distinct and recognizable style that sets you, the artist, apart from others in the NFT space.

      2. Convey a consistent artistic vision or message through their digital creations.

   B. Build an Online Presence

      1. Utilize social media platforms to showcase artwork, engage with followers, and build a community.

      2. Create a personal website or portfolio to display and sell digital art. This is in addition to listing your platform on an NFT marketplace.

   C. Embrace Collaboration and Networking

      1. Partner with other artists, influencers, or brands to create collaborative NFT projects or cross-promote each other's work.

      2. Participate in online forums and communities dedicated to digital art and NFTs to expand professional networks and learn from other artists.

D. Select the Right NFT Marketplace

1. Research various NFT marketplaces to find the one that best aligns with the artist's style, target audience, and values.

2. Evaluate factors such as platform fees, user experience, and support for eco-friendly practices.

3. Several NFT Marketplaces to consider:

a) OpenSea: OpenSea is one of the largest and most popular NFT marketplaces, featuring a wide range of digital assets, including art, collectibles, domain names, and virtual goods. It supports Ethereum and Polygon blockchains and offers an easy-to-use interface for both creators and collectors.

b) Rarible: Rarible is a decentralized NFT marketplace that allows users to create, buy, and sell digital art and collectibles. It features a user-friendly platform and offers a governance token (RARI) that enables its community to participate in decision-making processes.

c) SuperRare: SuperRare is a curated marketplace that focuses on high-quality, single-edition digital art. It has a rigorous selection process and is known for showcasing works by some of the top artists in the NFT space. The platform is built on the Ethereum blockchain.

d) Foundation: Foundation is another curated NFT marketplace that connects digital artists with collectors. It emphasizes creative innovation and supports a diverse range of artists, from emerging talents to established names. The platform operates on the Ethereum network.

e) Nifty Gateway: Nifty Gateway is a centralized NFT platform that hosts regular "drops" of exclusive, limited-edition digital art from renowned artists and brands. It offers a user-friendly experience and supports credit card payments, making it accessible to a broader audience beyond the crypto community.

f) Async Art: Async Art is a unique NFT platform that focuses on programmable art, allowing artists to create digital artworks with adjustable layers or elements. Collectors can own individual layers or elements of an artwork and modify them, resulting in dynamic and ever-evolving pieces.

g) KnownOrigin: KnownOrigin is a curated NFT platform that emphasizes high-quality digital art from both emerging and established artists. It operates on the Ethereum blockchain and offers a range of features, including auctions, editions, and artist collaborations.

h) Hic et Nunc (HEN): Hic et Nunc is an NFT platform built on the Tezos blockchain, known for its energy-efficient proof-of-stake consensus mechanism. It has a strong focus on sustainability and offers a simple interface for artists to mint and sell their digital creations.

4. These marketplaces offer various features, fees, and experiences, so artists and collectors should carefully consider which platform best aligns with their needs, preferences, and values before entering the NFT art world.

E. Pricing and Editions

1. Determine the appropriate pricing structure for digital art based on factors such as market demand, production costs, and the artist's reputation.

2. Consider the benefits of creating limited editions or one-of-a-kind pieces to enhance the perceived value and exclusivity of the artwork.

F. Marketing and Promotion

1. Leverage social media, email marketing, and public relations to generate buzz around NFT art releases.

2. Utilize data analytics to monitor the effectiveness of marketing efforts and adjust strategies accordingly.

II. Strategies for Collectors

A. Develop a Collection Strategy

1. Identify the collector's goals and motivations, such as financial gain, supporting emerging artists, or preserving cultural heritage.

2. Determine a focus or niche for the collection, such as a specific art style, theme, or artist.

B. Conduct Thorough Research

1. Investigate the background and credentials of artists before purchasing their digital art.

2. Analyze market trends and sales data to make informed decisions about which NFTs to acquire.

C. Engage with the Art Community

1. Participate in online forums, social media groups, and events dedicated to NFT art to expand knowledge and connections within the community.

2. Attend virtual exhibitions, auctions, and artist talks to stay informed about the latest developments in the NFT art world.

D. Ensure the Authenticity and Provenance of NFT Artworks

1. Verify the origin, ownership history, and smart contracts associated with NFTs before purchasing.

2. Consult with experts or utilizing third-party authentication services, if necessary.

E. Manage and Protect the NFT Collection

1. Select a secure digital wallet to store NFTs and safeguard private keys.

2. Regularly monitor the value of the collection and consider options for insurance or asset protection.

Summary

The advent of NFTs has undoubtedly disrupted the art world, introducing new opportunities for artists and collectors while also raising significant concerns and debates.

As the adoption of NFTs continues to grow, it is crucial for stakeholders to engage in ongoing conversations about the implications of this technology and its impact on the art world. Adopters of NFT also require a thoughtful strategy – where artists and collectors carefully select the right NFT marketplaces, developing the appropriate target audience and marketing strategies. Only by embracing both the benefits and addressing the controversies surrounding NFTs can the art world navigate the complex landscape of this digital revolution.

Entering the NFT art world can be both exciting and challenging for artists and collectors. By adopting the strategies outlined in this chapter, artists and collectors can better navigate the complexities of the NFT market, maximize their success, and contribute to the continued growth and evolution of digital art.

CHAPTER 5

The Gaming Industry and NFTs

The gaming industry has experienced a monumental shift in recent years, driven by rapid advancements in technology and the proliferation of the Internet. As games have grown in complexity and sophistication, the demand for unique and personalized in-game assets has also increased.

The implementation of non-fungible tokens (NFTs) in the gaming sector is a natural progression, providing a framework that can accommodate the needs of both developers and players alike. This use case for blockchain has caught fire, with over half of all blockchain activity coming from games and new games launching almost every day.

The vast majority of new blockchain game launches come from startups. Venture capital–backed studios with oftentimes zero games of their own, though frequently composed of at least one person with a background at a more traditional game studio, build a playable demo for a proposed game which integrates crypto and NFTs. Many of these get funded and then go on to launch games where the focus is often primarily on the tokenomics, giving gamers a way to earn money while trying to avoid a death spiral. Not all blockchain games follow this approach though.

© Ahmed Bouzid, Paolo Narciso, and Steve Wood 2023
A. Bouzid et al., *NFTs for Business*, https://doi.org/10.1007/978-1-4842-9777-3_5

Games' Approaches to NFTs

There are games which keep their focus on gameplay while integrating Web3 functions, some which add Web3 functions after having been released as a Web2 game for a while, and some where players wouldn't even be able to tell the game they're playing is Web3. Let's take a look at a few examples of each major implementation of blockchain into games.

A classic fully Web3 game would be Splinterlands. Splinterlands is a "card" game, similar to many other pure Web3 games; players build "decks" of "cards" representing different spells and creatures, which they use to battle other players in PvP turn-based combat. Cards can be upgraded over time with experience points and in-game resources. Each card is an NFT, meaning the entire core of the game is built around this technology.

Of course, when most people think of Web3 games, one of the first games which comes to mind is Sky Mavis' Axie Infinity. All the characters in this game, where players assemble teams of "Axies" to fight each other, are NFTs.

A different sort of game is Lords of Light, developed by Raini Studios and released in 2021 and had a collection of Web3 features included upon launch. This game is a mobile role-playing game (RPG) where players build kingdoms, collect and upgrade heroes within that kingdom, and battle other players in a medieval fantasy world with resources to collect, areas to explore, and quests to complete. The in-game currency for Lords of Light is Light tokens, but more importantly, the game uses NFTs for assets. The heroes, weapons, and armor that players collect are all NFTs, and other NFTs unlock access to special game features such as limited-time events.

Swords of Blood by Hit Box Games is another RPG-style game incorporating Web3 features like NFTs. It is an extension of a prior game by the same publisher called Blade Bound, which did not have any Web3 aspects at all and was entirely Web2. Swords of Blood takes that previously successful model and adds NFTs for high-value items, all housed within a wallet incorporated into the game. The Web2 model is still part of this game, but players start to accumulate NFTs and Web3 assets as they play.

NFT games aren't just an endeavor for smaller or niche studios though. Major brands and institutions are building experiences around them as well. World Cup AI League, developed by Altered State Machine, is one such example. This game, sponsored by none other than FIFA, has players assemble a team of four AI-powered players. The developers aim to integrate an NFT marketplace, after which all players and characters in the game will be NFTs. This game was designed with Web3 features in mind from the beginning, but initially released without them as the developers wanted to incorporate them later.

Square Enix is probably the biggest game developer to start building a game that incorporates NFTs. The game, Symbiogenesis, does not actually require a player to have any NFTs but have a degraded experience if they do not. Character NFTs enable players to read unique stories, gain experience fast, earn additional rewards from completing missions, create "replicas" of their characters, and more.

All these examples are mostly cases of trailblazers though – statistics on blockchain adoption in gaming show that it is far from universal. As of early 2023, a survey of game developers by industry conference group GDC indicated that roughly a quarter of game studios have any interest in developing blockchain-powered games, but only about 2% of studios are actively doing so. This figure represented a small decrease from the previous report issued in early 2022, which put the figure at around 27% for crypto and 28% for NFTs.

Many game developers and studios view blockchain as having no place in the gaming sector, a solution in search of a problem, strictly a vehicle for fraud, or even just an inferior way to do things when a centralized database can do the job. There is merit to these criticisms in many cases, and many of the scores of blockchain games that launch are poorly thought-out or raise red flags by focusing far too much on the blockchain aspects and not on the game aspects. That said, a proper implementation of assets like NFTs only serves to improve user experiences.

Publishers' Approaches to NFTs

The pro- and anti-blockchain/NFTs in gaming argument can be seen through the lens of two popular game stores: Steam and the Epic Games Store.

Game developer/publisher Valve imposed a blanket ban on all games that included blockchain or NFT technology in them from Steam, their game store. This was a major move considering that Steam is one of the primary ways desktop gamers find, purchase, download, and launch games. Despite this restriction, a few blockchain-powered games did persist on the platform.

The move was met with mixed responses. Though many in the community praised the decision, Valve was accused of simply trying to eliminate the existence of game marketplaces powered by NFTs where they couldn't earn a cut, including by one developer whose game was purged from the platform. Valve's president claimed they did this because while blockchain is a great technology, "the ways in which has been utilized are currently are all pretty sketchy" and that "people who are currently active in that space are not usually good actors."

One Web3 game publisher, Gala Games, listed one of its games on Steam by removing all NFT functionality from the game in that version of it. This allows them to onboard players from Steam's ecosystem then migrate them to an internal system in the future so those players can gain the fullest experience.

On the other side of the spectrum, Epic Games welcomes NFTs in its Epic Games Store. Their CEO stated that he believes "stores and operating system makers shouldn't interfere [with developer choices in how to build games] by forcing their views onto others" and followed up that Epic certainly would not be doing that.

Considering Epic Games developed and launched Fortnite, one of the biggest success stories in gaming history, this shows how polarized major actors in the industry are when it comes to NFTs. The Epic Games

Store is much smaller than Steam, but could end up benefiting as one of the biggest game libraries which permits NFT-powered products. Gala Games has indicated that it intends to publish its releases there, and the platform published its first banner NFT title called Blankos Block Party, produced by Mythical Games which is valued at over $1bn as of its last funding round.

It's clear that publishers, studios, and other gaming platforms are adopting this technology. It's also clear that interest in doing so varies greatly between highly enthusiastic and diametrically opposed. With only 1 in 50 studios currently building NFT-powered games and 75% of the industry having zero interest in considering it, the value of using blockchain technology still needs to be proven before widespread adoption can ensue.

The trepidation caused by NFTs' poor reputation needs to be overcome, possibly through rehabilitation of rebranding, if the industry is to take advantage of the benefits the technology can bring. The legacy of "rug pulls" and abandoned projects leaves many people skeptical at best and hostile at worst toward even the idea of building or playing an NFT game. Developers often vocally support the possibilities and ideals of what NFTs can do for gaming, but often cannot embrace those due to their tainted legacy.

Fixing this issue requires an infrastructure and a commitment to quality by developers who leverage blockchain technology without making it the forefront of what they create. Similar to how nobody thinks about how Fortnite requires an always-on Internet connection when they play the game, at least until they lag or lose service, games need to integrate blockchain in ways that allow players to enjoy their experience without thinking about how they are using those protocols. Once this has been overcome, hesitancy is sure to drop off as well.

Benefits of Blockchain Gaming

The benefits blockchain and NFTs can bring to games are quite substantial, when properly implemented.

Having an immutable record of transactions, transferrable unique assets, decentralized storage, and cross-platform portability offers numerous benefits to games, gamers, and game developers.

One example is verifiable ownership. Blockchain's ability to create an immutable record of transactions allows for the clear establishment of ownership of in-game assets. For gamers, this means that they can prove they own the digital items they have acquired, which is crucial for trading, selling, or transferring these assets, especially if they wish to do this outside of the closed environment provided by a game's creators.

This can be seen in Star Atlas' record of asset ownership being public. Anyone can check the leaderboards at any time and see exactly who owns what. As of this writing, the top player has $654,844 and anyone can click on their page to verify exactly what those assets are. That person can then check the marketplace and see exactly what those assets are currently trading for and act on that information.

This function prevents people who want to buy an asset from getting ripped off and ensures those who want to sell an asset get exactly what it is worth. Furthermore, the verifiability means asset provenance can be traced. If someone in this game owns a star cruiser which participated in a particularly famous battle, for example, it may be worth more than the basic trading price for other versions of that asset and command a premium.

Developers also benefit from this verifiable ownership. They can track the distribution of in-game assets and enable transfers outside their cloistered ecosystems while still reaping benefits such as those provided by royalties. This helps prevent fraudulent activities and ensure the game's economy remains balanced. They can monitor transactions of their assets and verify that everything is above board if a dispute arises, even outside of their own markets.

This is in stark contrast to the cloistered systems of Web2 gaming, where nobody can take anything they buy anywhere else. A real-world analogy to the benefits this provides can be found by imagining a person who buys a car, but they are only able to use it on roads built by the car dealer and can only sell it on the car dealer's lot if they're able to sell it at all. This would make cars effectively equivalent to go-karts at a go-kart track, even though you're "buying" it. NFTs remove this restriction.

Trust is essential in online environments where players and developers need to have confidence in the system's integrity. Because blockchains ensure transaction records cannot be manipulated or altered by a single entity, they provide a higher level of security and trust than a centralized database. Even in the case of a blockchain hack, past records can never be altered. This trust fosters a more vibrant gaming community. It also encourages players to buy more digital assets, especially since they can take them off the proverbial go-kart track.

Since Web3 assets, specifically NFTs, are more akin to buying a car you can take anywhere as opposed to metaphorical Web2 assets you buy and have to leave at the track, Web3 enables far superior asset exchanges among gamers. They disintermediate transactions and provide a transparent transaction history, reducing the risk of fraud for anyone who does a modicum of research into what they're buying.

This efficiency encourages the growth of in-game economies and further incentivizes player participation.

Decentralized marketplaces like OpenSea allow users to trade various NFT-based in-game assets, including those from games like Decentraland and Axie Infinity. Gamers are not restricted to using the marketplaces created by the game developers themselves. Though gamers may find these specialized platforms more suited for transactions specific to a given game, the open nature of the ecosystem means players are not locked in, which forces all parties to behave more honestly and maintain high standards.

There are several other advantages blockchains offer games centralized systems, particularly in terms of security and censorship resistance.

Centralized databases are more susceptible to attacks due to their single point of failure. Should a hacker gain access to a central server, they can manipulate and compromise the entire system. In contrast, since blockchain technology runs on decentralized networks, they're more resistant to such attacks. Since the data is stored across multiple nodes, compromising the system requires enormous computational power and coordination, making it much more challenging for malicious actors to breach the network.

Security and Censorship Resistance

Security concerns are not eliminated by using blockchain solutions though as putting something on-chain does not render it immune to attack. The attack vectors change. The Ronin Bridge hack serves as a cautionary example of security vulnerabilities in decentralized systems.

The Ronin Bridge is a blockchain platform used by Axie Infinity which allows users to transfer assets between the Ethereum network and the Ronin sidechain, created by Axie Infinity developer Sky Mavis to facilitate a more streamlined experience for people playing their games.

In March 2022, the Ronin Bridge experienced a security breach in which an amount of cryptocurrency which was at the time valued around $625 million was stolen by hackers. The attackers exploited a vulnerability in the platform's multisig wallet system, which required signatures from multiple wallets to authorize transactions.

This incident highlights the reality that even blockchain-based systems can be vulnerable to attacks if not adequately secured. The breach underscores the importance of robust security measures and ongoing vigilance to identify and address potential vulnerabilities in both centralized and decentralized systems.

In this case, the vulnerability was not inherent to the blockchain technology itself but rather in the implementation of the multisig wallet system. Therefore, it is crucial for developers to adopt best practices in security and engage in regular audits to ensure the safety of their platforms.

One of the few cases where NFTs were lost during a hack, and not a scam or a phishing attack, was the "Sturmer" hack in 2021. In this attack, a hacker was able to steal over $600,000 worth of NFTs from the Nifty Gateway NFT marketplace. However, it's worth noting that the hacker did so by exploiting a vulnerability in the website's authentication system rather than by exploiting the blockchain or relevant smart contracts themselves.

To mitigate risks and enhance security in blockchain-based systems, developers and operators should consider the following measures:

- Regularly audit smart contracts and platform code: Conducting exhaustive reviews of smart contracts and platform code can identify and address vulnerabilities before they can be exploited.

- Correctly implementing multisig wallets and secure authorization mechanisms: Multisig wallets can provide an additional layer of security when correctly implemented and maintained by requiring multiple signatures to authorize transactions.

- Employing decentralized security solutions: Decentralized security solutions, such as decentralized autonomous organizations (DAOs), may in some cases improve protocol security by distributing control and decision-making across a larger group of participants.

- Education and awareness: Ensure all participants in a given ecosystem, from developers to users, are aware of potential security risks and best practices can help mitigate the likelihood of successful attacks.

While the Ronin Bridge hack shows blockchain-based systems can be vulnerable to security breaches, recall that these incidents are the result of specific vulnerabilities in the implementation or management of the system, rather than inherent flaws in the technology itself. Adopting best security practices and maintaining vigilance can help developers ensure their blockchain-based platforms remain secure and resistant to attacks.

Security issues aside, censorship resistance is one of the most touted benefits of blockchain, and consequently NFTs. The benefits of this popular feature are not lost on the gaming sector.

Being resistant to censorship promotes a more equitable, open, and democratic environment for gamers and developers alike, which has contributed to the growing adoption of NFTs in the industry. Decentralization is one of the key aspects of NFTs, and with all blockchain technology more broadly.

Unlike traditional centralized gaming platforms where a single entity, usually the game developer, wields significant power over the game's assets and rules, NFT-based games distribute control across the network. This decentralized structure makes it more difficult for any single party to censor or manipulate in-game assets or economies, resulting in a more fair and transparent gaming experience.

However, the full benefit of this technology requires that developers themselves surrender control of the core game itself. If they do not, then the usability of a given in-game asset can be diluted by altering other aspects of the game. This poses an issue though, as game developers today are far less likely to relinquish control over their games than they were in an era where the final shipped version of a game was complete. Gaming today is fraught with developers who publish quickly, then patch and add downloadable content (DLC) which requires players to continually accept changes to their games. This fact of modern game development limits the usefulness of NFTs in these sorts of environments.

Another example of the advantages of censorship resistance is how NFTs enable true digital ownership of in-game assets. Gamers can buy, sell, or trade these assets without requiring approval from a central authority. This freedom to transact without censorship or interference encourages greater levels of creativity and innovation within the gaming community, such as through modding or "create-to-earn"–focused games, as players have the autonomy to use and monetize their assets as they see fit. This aspect of NFTs is particularly appealing to game developers who want to create player-driven economies and empower their users, as these players know their creations will not be "censored" by others and in fact can even be traded freely outside the closed game ecosystem.

Interoperability and Monetization

NFTs have the potential to be interoperable across different gaming platforms and even across different games. This means that gamers can, in theory at least, transfer their NFT-based in-game assets from one platform or game to another, without the risk of censorship or restrictions imposed by centralized authorities. This is one of the most frequently cited benefits of NFTs in gaming. In practice, this requires some form of common protocol or network shared by games that enables them to properly interpret and contextualize assets that are not native to a given game.

This feature has the potential to revolutionize the gaming industry by fostering a more open and interconnected ecosystem, which in turn encourages game developers to adopt NFTs to stay competitive and provide a better user experience. There are projects working to develop these common protocols, and Sony filed a patent application in July 2021 for related NFT technologies, indicating that both startup entrepreneurs and entrenched industry giants alike are moving to build out these solutions.

Another benefit delivered by the censorship resistance of NFTs is the increased freedom of expression for both gamers and game developers. The decentralized nature of NFTs allows for a more diverse range of in-game assets and experiences, as creators can develop content without fear of censorship from centralized gatekeepers. This ties back to the concept of "create-to-earn," where modders and other independent actors can express themselves by creating items for in-game environments and share them with their respective communities as a form of self-expression.

This freedom can lead to more innovative and varied gaming experiences, attracting a broader audience and fostering a more vibrant and inclusive gaming community. One lens through which we can see how self-expression is highly valued by gamers and developers is through that of "avatar skins."

Avatar skins are a prime example of unique and personalized in-game assets that have experienced a surge in demand in recent years. These skins, which are simply cosmetic changes to a player's virtual character that have little if any impact on gameplay, have gained immense popularity for several reasons.

Avatar skins enable players to express their identity and style within the gaming world. As online gaming communities grow, gamers often view their avatars as extensions of their personalities. This is even more true in online environments like metaverses, where individual gamers interact with the digital world in ways which resemble real-life interactions.

Customizing their virtual characters with unique skins allows players to showcase their individuality and make a statement about their tastes, preferences, or affiliations. By doing so, they create a sense of belonging and connection with other like-minded players in the community.

These skins can also serve as a symbol of social status and achievement within the gaming community.

Some skins are exclusively available through in-game accomplishments, special promotions, or limited-time events. Owning a rare or highly sought-after skin can signal a player's dedication, skill, or commitment to the game. This exclusivity often fuels the desire for unique avatar skins, as they can be seen as a reflection of a player's standing and reputation within the community. Furthermore, demand for avatar skins directly correlates with increases in the value of virtual goods.

Many games have established marketplaces where players can buy, sell, or trade their in-game assets, including avatar skins. With the introduction of NFTs, these skins can be tokenized and traded on various platforms, providing gamers opportunities to monetize their assets.

The potential for profit, coupled with the rarity and aesthetic appeal of certain skins, further drives the demand for unique avatar skins. Thus, the censorship resistance and security aspects of NFTs make for a natural marriage with avatar skins. This makes games more appealing to developers and studios as players can spend their money knowing they will be able to resell their valuable skin, or take it elsewhere, if their interests change.

The resistance to censorship that NFTs specifically, and blockchain more generally, provide has significant implications for the gaming sector. The decentralized control, true digital ownership, cross-platform compatibility, and freedom of expression offered by NFTs create a more open, fair, and democratic environment for gamers and developers.

This has been recognized by both groups, which is a major reason driving adoption of NFTs within the gaming industry – they offer a more appealing and empowering alternative to traditional centralized gaming platforms. Even developers who shy away from NFTs generally align with the philosophies the technology supports; they avoid them for other reasons which must be addressed in other ways.

For those developers who have taken steps to adopt NFTs within their products, two primary beneficial factors have facilitated this process: the ability to tokenize in-game assets and the potential for the creation of decentralized gaming ecosystems.

The tokenization of in-game assets, such as characters, weapons, or virtual real estate, enables the conversion of these digital items into unique, tradable tokens on the blockchain. This is what allows for verifiable ownership and creates the ability to transfer assets between users or across different gaming platforms. In essence, tokenization provides a degree of interoperability that has been previously unattainable in the gaming industry.

This has substantial value, though many game developers studiously avoid acknowledging it out of fear that they will lose control or revenues. The revenue issue is very easy to address, but the control issue is another matter since developers must ship more-or-less fully complete games if they incorporate NFTs into them, or at least commit to not changing many things post-release.

Decentralized gaming ecosystems offer a profound opportunity for the utilization of NFTs and blockchain technology within the gaming industry. While it may not be desirable in every instance, leveraging decentralized autonomous organizations (DAOs), smart contracts, and decentralized applications (dApps) can herald a new paradigm of gaming in which the community has direct influence over the development and governance of the game itself. Community-run games and development platforms can spring into existence in ways not possible before.

With the introduction of decentralized finance (DeFi) and the metaverse, gaming platforms can further capitalize on the potential of NFTs. Gamers can now participate in DeFi activities, such as lending, borrowing, and staking, using their in-game assets as collateral. This financial integration provides an additional layer of value and utility to in-game assets, making them even more appealing to gamers and developers alike. Of course, this does create risk on several levels, which is one of the reasons many developers shy away from incorporating blockchain technologies into their games as it is what brings the unsavory actors into the space and creates the bad reputation.

Furthermore, the metaverse concept, an interconnected virtual universe that transcends individual gaming platforms, creates an opportunity for seamless integration of NFTs across different games and virtual worlds. By enabling the portability of in-game assets and avatars, NFTs can facilitate new forms of interaction and collaboration among gamers, further deepening their engagement with the gaming world.

Review

As the adoption of NFTs continues to grow in the gaming industry, we can expect an acceleration in the development of Web3-based gaming platforms. These platforms will harness the full potential of blockchain technology, providing gamers and developers with enhanced security, trust, and creative freedom. In doing so, they will set the stage for a new era in gaming, one that is characterized by the convergence of decentralized technologies and the limitless possibilities they offer.

For gamers, the primary advantage of NFTs is the ability to truly own, control, and monetize their in-game assets. Traditional gaming systems often restrict the transfer of in-game items or the monetization of assets outside the game environment. However, with NFTs, gamers can trade or sell their unique digital assets on various marketplaces, allowing them to capitalize on the value they have created within the game. This added level of control and ownership can lead to greater long-term engagement and investment in the gaming ecosystem.

Another benefit for gamers is the potential for earning passive income through the use of their NFT-based in-game assets. As mentioned earlier, DeFi integration allows gamers to participate in various financial activities, such as staking or lending, using their NFTs as collateral. This financial participation can generate a passive income stream, incentivizing gamers to continue engaging with the game and accumulating valuable assets.

For game developers, the use of NFTs and blockchain technology can lead to new revenue streams and enhanced player retention. By tokenizing in-game assets and allowing for their sale on secondary markets, developers can earn a percentage of each transaction, providing a continuous source of income. Additionally, the integration of DeFi elements into the gaming platform can create novel financial opportunities for developers, such as in-game asset lending or yield farming.

Another advantage for developers is the potential for cost reduction and efficiency gains through the utilization of blockchain technology. By leveraging smart contracts, developers can automate various aspects of the gaming environment, such as the creation, distribution, and management of in-game assets. This automation can lead to reduced operational costs, as well as enhanced security and transparency throughout the gaming ecosystem.

Moreover, the use of NFTs can help foster a sense of community and loyalty among players. When players have a vested interest in the in-game assets they own, they are more likely to remain engaged and active within the game world. This increased level of commitment can lead to greater player retention and, ultimately, higher revenues for developers.

The adoption of NFTs and blockchain technology in the gaming industry is poised to transform the landscape in numerous ways. As we look to the future, several key areas will likely experience significant disruption and innovation as a result of this integration.

First, the concept of cross-platform gaming and interoperability will become increasingly relevant. As NFTs enable the seamless transfer of in-game assets between different gaming platforms and virtual worlds, gamers will enjoy a more cohesive and interconnected experience. This shift toward a unified gaming ecosystem will promote collaboration and competition across various platforms, further driving innovation and creativity within the industry.

Second, the rise of decentralized gaming platforms and community-driven development will democratize the creation and governance of games. Gamers will have the opportunity to participate in the decision-making processes surrounding game development and updates, leading to a more inclusive and player-centric gaming environment. This increased level of collaboration between gamers and developers will foster innovation and ensure that games continue to evolve in response to player preferences and feedback.

Lastly, the integration of DeFi elements and the expansion of the metaverse will lead to new economic opportunities and business models within the gaming industry. As the line between the virtual and real-world economy continues to blur, gaming platforms will become hubs for digital asset creation, trade, and investment. This convergence of gaming and finance will redefine the gaming landscape, creating a new era of interconnectedness and value creation for gamers and developers alike.

Summary

The adoption of NFTs and blockchain technology in the gaming industry presents a multitude of opportunities for both gamers and developers. As these technologies become more deeply ingrained in the fabric of the gaming world, we can expect to see a paradigm shift toward a more decentralized, interconnected, and economically vibrant gaming ecosystem as well as completely different settings such as music.

1. `https://wp.dappradar.com/wp-content/uploads/2022/09/dappradar.com-aug-industry-report-compressed.pdf`

2. `https://images.reg.techweb.com/Web/UBMTechweb/%7Bc64eb256-440f-4c4c-8b63-9e190c967b35%7D_GDC23_SOTI_Report_r1.pdf`

3. www.eurogamer.net/gabe-newell-explains-why-
    steam-banned-nfts

4. https://patentscope.wipo.int/search/en/
    detail.jsf?docId=US378324956

CHAPTER 6

The Music Industry and NFTs

The concept of NFTs in music, or "music NFTs," offers an innovative approach to digitizing and monetizing music. A music NFT isn't merely a digitized track or album; it is a digital token that can represent ownership or proof of authenticity of a musical work. But, the melody of NFTs doesn't stop at just tokenizing music.

While the term "music NFT" may imply a focus solely on music, the scope of these digital tokens expands beyond the audio. A music NFT could include a variety of components such as the following:

1. Tracks or albums: The most obvious choice. Musicians can tokenize their tracks or full albums, representing a direct purchase of their music from fans.

2. Artwork and visual components: Album covers, promotional graphics, or any associated visual art can be tokenized as part of the NFT. For instance, Kings of Leon included exclusive artwork as part of their NFT album release.

© Ahmed Bouzid, Paolo Narciso, and Steve Wood 2023
A. Bouzid et al., *NFTs for Business*, https://doi.org/10.1007/978-1-4842-9777-3_6

3. Exclusive rights and experiences: Musicians can include special privileges, like VIP concert tickets, backstage passes, or the rights to future music releases within the NFT. This enhances the value proposition for fans, making the NFT about more than just music.

4. Creative assets: Think of stems, song lyrics, or unpublished demos. Musicians can include these unique elements as part of their NFTs, offering fans a peek into their creative process.

In essence, a music NFT serves as a digital collector's item, imbued with elements that make it unique and valuable. From a musician's perspective, NFTs offer an avenue for direct engagement with fans and a potentially lucrative form of monetization. From a fan's viewpoint, music NFTs provide exclusive access to their favorite artists' work and experiences, making them part of a unique community.

Yet, as with any innovation, music NFTs come with their own set of challenges, including environmental concerns due to energy consumption of blockchain transactions, copyright issues, and market volatility. It's crucial that musicians, industry professionals, and enthusiasts navigate this emerging landscape with knowledge, understanding, and a pinch of caution.

The music industry, for all its glitz and glamor, has long been a challenging space for artists. For decades, musicians have struggled with issues of control, compensation, and connection with fans. The digital revolution, while making music more accessible, brought its own complexities. Low royalties from streaming, piracy, and the saturation of digital platforms left many artists struggling. But then, a new note started playing in this symphony – the note of non-fungible tokens (NFTs).

NFTs and the Music Industry: An Evolving Love Story

NFTs, unique digital assets on the blockchain, are changing the game by creating a new avenue for artists to release their music, interact with fans, and generate income. While the concept might sound like it jumped out of a cyberpunk novel, it's very much a reality. The adoption of NFTs by the music industry, despite being in its early days, is creating ripples of change.

One of the first major instances of this adoption came from Kings of Leon, an American rock band known for hits like "Use Somebody" and "Sex on Fire." They hit a milestone in the music industry by being the first band to release an album as an NFT, titled "When You See Yourself." Their NFT release comprised three types of tokens – one offered special album packages, another offered unique experiences like front-row concert seats for life, and the third featured exclusive audiovisual art. This was not just a sale; it was a statement, a testament to the promise of NFTs in empowering artists.

DJ and music producer 3LAU (pronounced "Blau") also made headlines, not just for adopting NFTs, but for the mind-boggling amount he generated from them. He sold an album via NFTs for a staggering $11.6 million, earning more than he might have through traditional routes. Following this, he created history by selling the first-ever NFT-backed music festival tickets for his own music festival "Ultraviolet."

The NFT revolution is not limited to established artists. Independent musicians, such as Grammy-winning producer RAC, are using NFTs to connect with their fan base directly bypassing traditional industry intermediaries. RAC believes that music is the most undervalued sector in the world today – and he believes he can change it with Web3. By tokenizing his $RAC and a limited-edition cassette tape, he offered his fans unique memorabilia and a piece of his creative journey.

The growing number of musicians turning toward NFTs is proof of an ongoing paradigm shift. From offering an immersive fan experience to providing a more lucrative and control-oriented avenue for artists, NFTs are slowly but surely making their mark on the music industry.

While the adoption of NFTs might seem exciting, one might ask – why the fuss? The answer lies in the manifold benefits NFTs offer both musicians and fans.

For Musicians: Control, Compensation, and Connection

One of the most significant advantages of NFTs for musicians is control. In a traditional setting, artists often cede a considerable amount of control to record labels, distributors, and streaming platforms. NFTs provide artists with the power to control their distribution, valuing their work, and their relationship with fans.

Control is not only about distribution; it extends to compensation as well. NFTs allow artists to set their price for their work, a luxury often unavailable in traditional contracts. Artists can also program royalties into their tokens, ensuring they receive a percentage of future resales – a feature that recognizes the enduring value of the artist to their work. This is a revolutionary feature, particularly in an industry where artists receive a minuscule fraction from the resale of their work, especially in the secondary market.

The benefits extend beyond control and compensation to the third crucial "C" – connection. NFTs enable artists to interact directly with their fans. They can offer unique experiences and exclusives that go beyond conventional merchandise or VIP packages. This could be anything from unreleased tracks, limited-edition album artwork, virtual concert tickets, or even interactions with the artists themselves. This direct connection not only enhances fan engagement but also fosters a sense of community and belonging.

For Fans: Exclusivity, Ownership, and Investment

For fans, NFTs are a gateway to a more immersive and engaging music experience. The exclusivity that NFTs offer is unparalleled. Owning a unique digital asset like a limited-edition album cover or a virtual concert ticket makes the fan experience more personal and memorable.

Ownership of music has seen a decline in the age of streaming services. NFTs bring back that sense of ownership, but with a digital twist. By owning an NFT, fans hold a piece of their favorite artist's legacy, a digital asset that they can showcase, trade, or even resell.

Moreover, NFTs turn fandom into a potential investment. As the value of an artist's NFT rises, so does the value of the tokens held by fans. This makes being a fan not just emotionally rewarding, but potentially financially rewarding as well.

NFTs can shift power dynamics by offering artists more control over their work, their earnings, and their relationship with fans. This shift could lead to a future music landscape where artists are less dependent on record labels, distributors, and other intermediaries – an industry where musicians can create on their terms, reach out to fans directly, and receive fair compensation for their work.

The advent of NFTs in the music industry is akin to the introduction of the electric guitar in rock music – it has the potential to redefine norms and reshape the industry.

Shifting Power Dynamics and Redefining Fan Culture

This shift in power dynamics also promises a more participatory fan culture. As fans invest in an artist's NFTs, they become stakeholders with a vested interest in the artist's success. This could lead to a deeper connection between artists and fans, fostering a sense of community and shared success.

But like any new technology, NFTs bring uncertainties alongside opportunities. Questions around the environmental impact of blockchain, copyright issues, and market volatility are still being ironed out. It's also essential to ensure that the benefits of NFTs reach all artists, not just the well-established or tech-savvy ones.

However, as we've seen from our case studies, many artists and fans are willing to navigate these challenges. They are eager to explore the exciting possibilities NFTs offer – of a music industry that's more empowering, equitable, and engaging.

While the recent symphony between NFTs and the music industry has been playing an exhilarating tune, it's important to acknowledge that every composition has its discordant notes. This emerging technology, for all its revolutionary potential, does come with its pitfalls and challenges. Let's delve into this less harmonious side of the NFT revolution in the music industry.

The most glaring pitfall revolves around the issue of access and equity. The current wave of NFT adoption in the music industry has largely been driven by well-established artists or those with a robust understanding of blockchain technology. This raises the question of accessibility and fairness for all artists. Can smaller, independent, or less tech-savvy artists also benefit from NFTs? Or does the current scenario risk creating another elite tier within the music industry?

For example, when the rock band Kings of Leon released their album as an NFT, it drew mixed reactions. Some hailed it as a groundbreaking move; others saw it as a venture that only well-established artists could afford to take. The hefty price of creating and selling NFTs, plus the cost of understanding and navigating this new space, is a barrier for many musicians.

Another pitfall is the volatility and speculative nature of the NFT market. While the stories of musicians making millions from their NFTs are impressive, they might not reflect the experience of every artist. Much like any market tied to cryptocurrencies, the value of NFTs can fluctuate drastically. This volatility may not bode well for artists looking for a stable income source. But this risk is not unlike any other album that a musician releases if no one buys it. These sorts of NFTs are probably less susceptible to NFT hype cycles because it's not pure speculation like a Bored Ape or a CryptoPunk – music NFTs actually have something behind them.

A case in point is the DJ and music producer 3LAU, who sold an album for a staggering $11.6 million via NFTs. However, such a high-value transaction could raise fans' expectations for subsequent NFT releases. If the market faces a downturn, and NFTs don't fetch the same high prices, it might lead to disappointment or financial losses for both artists and fans.

The environmental impact of NFTs is another pitfall that can't be overlooked. NFTs, like other applications of blockchain technology, have a substantial carbon footprint due to the energy-intensive processes involved in mining and trading. This has led to criticism from environmentally conscious fans and artists, posing a challenge to the widespread adoption of NFTs in the music industry.

A noteworthy case is the band Massive Attack, who, despite embracing NFTs, have raised concerns about their environmental impact. They are now working on a project with researchers from the Tyndall Centre for Climate Change Research to reduce the carbon footprint of touring and releasing music via NFTs. However, not all artists might have the resources or expertise to undertake such initiatives.

Developing the Strategy

The digital orchestra of non-fungible tokens (NFTs) in the music industry has opened a new frontier for musicians, bands, and promoters alike. But, stepping into the world of NFTs requires more than just enthusiasm; it demands strategic planning, understanding of the technology, and awareness of the associated risks. Let's explore a potential strategy for leveraging NFTs in the music industry and ways to mitigate associated risks.

Defining the NFT Opportunity

Before diving headfirst into the world of NFTs, musicians and promoters need to define the opportunity. What does success look like? Is it just about generating additional income, or is it about fostering a deeper connection with fans? Or perhaps, it's about gaining more control over music distribution and valuing the artist's work.

Kings of Leon found the opportunity in providing special album packages, unique experiences like front-row concert seats for life, and exclusive audiovisual art through their NFTs. Meanwhile, independent musicians like RAC see the opportunity in directly connecting with their fan base, bypassing traditional industry intermediaries.

Crafting an NFT Strategy

Once the opportunity is defined, the next step is to craft an effective NFT strategy. This strategy should consider several factors:

1. Identify what you want to tokenize: You could tokenize a full album, a single track, concert tickets, or even unique experiences. The key is to offer something that fans will value and that captures your artistic identity.

2. Choose the right platform: There are several NFT marketplaces, each with its unique features and audience. Some popular ones include OpenSea, Rarible, and Foundation. It's important to research each platform's fee structures, user-friendliness, and audience demographics to find the one that suits your needs the best.

3. Price your NFT wisely: Pricing is a delicate balance. It should be high enough to reflect the value of the artist's work but not so high as to deter potential buyers. Remember that fans are not just buying music or art; they are buying a piece of someone's legacy.

4. Promote your NFT: An NFT is only as successful as its reach. Use your social media channels, newsletters, and other marketing platforms to build awareness and hype around your NFT drop. You could even use traditional media outlets or PR agencies for broader reach.

5. Engage with your fans: NFTs offer a unique opportunity to engage directly with your fans. Make this engagement count. Offer them insights into your creative process, exclusive previews, or just a thank you note for their support.

Considering the Risks and Mitigating Them

While the benefits of NFTs are enticing, it's important to consider the associated risks and take steps to alleviate them.

1. Market volatility: Like any market linked to cryptocurrencies, the NFT market can be volatile. It's essential to not stake your entire livelihood on the success of your NFTs. Diversify your income sources and ensure you have a steady revenue stream independent of your NFT sales.

2. Technological barriers: Navigating the world of blockchain and NFTs can be daunting for those unfamiliar with the technology. Collaborate with technology experts or hire professionals who can guide you through the process.

3. Legal issues: It's crucial to understand the legal implications of selling NFTs, particularly around intellectual property rights and royalty arrangements. Bored Apes leaned into this by offering full IP rights to anyone who owns an Ape. Consulting with legal professionals will help protect your rights and interests.

4. Environmental impact: The carbon footprint of NFTs, due to the energy-intensive processes of blockchain, is a genuine concern. Artists can alleviate this by choosing more eco-friendly blockchain platforms, offsetting their carbon emissions, or contributing a portion of their NFT sales to environmental causes.

Music NFT Marketplaces to Consider (as of 2023)

The landscape for NFTS in music is rapidly evolving. If you are pursuing an NFT strategy for your music, you may want to consider the platform to use and understand both its strengths and limitations. Here are some platforms that you may consider:

1. OpenSea: As one of the most versatile and user-friendly NFT marketplaces, OpenSea is highly favored among artists. Its flexibility to handle a wide range of digital assets, including music, art, domain names, and virtual goods, gives artists ample room

for creative expression. OpenSea also boasts an expansive user base, increasing artists' potential reach and marketability. Kings of Leon leveraged OpenSea to release their NFT albums, making it a well-trusted platform in the music industry.

2. Async Art: Async Art focuses on "programmable art," which includes music. The unique feature here is the ability to create layered NFTs where each layer can be controlled independently, allowing for interactivity and dynamic change over time. This opens up new possibilities for musicians to create programmable music, where different aspects of a track can be owned and controlled by different people.

3. PlayTreks: PlayTreks is a music platform offering a 360-degree view of song data analytics across various platforms, including streaming services, social media, and online music stores. By introducing NFTs, PlayTreks allows artists to tokenize their music and reap the financial benefits directly, without intermediaries. Its comprehensive analytics can provide valuable insights into the reach and impact of an artist's work, informing their strategy and marketing.

4. One of: One of is a green NFT platform built specifically for the music community. Its focus is on making NFTs affordable and accessible to all artists and fans, with minting costs reportedly 97% less than on Ethereum. OneOf has also partnered with environmental organizations to offset its carbon footprint, which could make it an appealing choice for environmentally conscious artists.

5. TuneGoNFT: TuneGoNFT is a platform that focuses on connecting artists directly with their fans via NFTs. The platform is designed to allow artists to tokenize their music, merchandise, and experiences and then sell them to their fans. TuneGoNFT 's focus on creating a direct artist-to-fan connection can help artists foster deeper engagement with their fan base.

6. AirNFTs: AirNFTs is a platform where anyone can create, buy, and sell NFTs. For musicians, this means an accessible way to tokenize their music and sell it directly to fans. The platform provides a streamlined process for minting NFTs and offers tools to promote artists' work, making it a favorable platform for artists new to the NFT space.

7. Onlymusix: Onlymusix presents a specialized platform for musicians, where artists can mint and sell their NFTs. It offers solutions for artists to monetize their music, live concerts, merchandise, and more. Its focus on the music industry makes it a highly relevant choice for artists looking to capitalize on the NFT wave in a space dedicated to their craft.

Each platform provides its unique spin on the intersection of NFTs and music, catering to different needs and priorities of artists. Whether it's the versatility of OpenSea, the programmable art concept of Async, or the green and accessible approach of OneOf, these platforms are paving the way for artists to explore, innovate, and thrive in the new digital economy of music.

Summary

Music NFTs represent a new verse in the ongoing song of music evolution. They offer exciting possibilities by fusing music, art, technology, and fan engagement. While we are only at the cusp of understanding their full potential, one thing is clear – music NFTs are striking a chord that's too compelling to ignore. As we dance to this digital rhythm, it is crucial to keep adapting, exploring, and innovating. After all, isn't that what music is all about?

CHAPTER 7

Other Use Cases

In this chapter, our aim is twofold: first, to propose a methodology for identifying how this exotic thing called an NFT can be used in the real world to solve real problems, and second, to apply this methodology to explain and surface the value that NFTs are delivering and can deliver in five "real-life" sectors: event ticketing, food and drink, fashion, financial loans, and supply chain management.

Understanding NFTs

When someone encounters the word "NFT" today, as of this time of writing in mid-2023, in the crushing majority of cases their reaction is one of two: either they have never heard the word at all or have heard it but have no idea what it means (three out of four people in the United States fall into this category),[1] or they have heard it, understand it to a nontrivial extent, but believe that it is a tool that one uses in the context of digital visual art – images or videos that one stamps with some digitally created and tracked identifier to render unique that piece of digital artifact within a community of other like-minded people who take seriously the notion that because something digital is rendered unique, it is valuable and worth paying *real* money for. Do NFTs *do* anything beyond help facilitate a game of digital pretend, where as soon as the people gathered were to stop pretending, the NFT, the coins, the tokens, and the ledger, used to keep track of this

---

[1] https://money.com/people-know-what-nft-is/

© Ahmed Bouzid, Paolo Narciso, and Steve Wood 2023
A. Bouzid et al., *NFTs for Business*, https://doi.org/10.1007/978-1-4842-9777-3_7

and that, go away in a puff, leaving no trace other than the real-life damage resulting from the real money and time and energy and emotion lost propping up the game? The answer – for those who have understood enough of NFT to be able to come up with the question – is a "no." NFTs are essentially a scam, according to them, a sham, a big delusional house of pretend cards that is sure to come down crashing, sooner or later. This is where the vast, vast majority of real people who live in real life and deal with real problems stand today when it comes to NFTs.

Those who do understand NFTs and who do take them seriously have a good answer to this witheringly skeptical perspective. They note that what we call real money is also a big giant pretend game, so is the consent that we give to the authorities that manage the game, so is everything else that complex, modern life relies on: from norms to ethical standards, to moral infrastructures and even taboos. None of it is any more "real," less susceptible to immediate vanishing, than any of the instruments used in the digital world. It takes one loss of faith event in a currency by enough people, and that currency will collapse, with that initial loss of faith within a small number of panicked skeptics creating an epidemic of faithlessness. And once the currency has lost the confidence of those who use it, it becomes instantly useless – the same with the leader of a country – even one who has under their command all the generals and all the weaponry that come with it, or a mayor, or a teacher, or a spiritual leader, or an influencer. Should enough people decide to withdraw their assent for something, the value of that something, no matter how tangible in real life may be, will vanish into thin air, its erstwhile seeming solidity now revealed to be a mirage sustained by a tacit collective agreement that gave it a place and a name and a set of functions in our ontology of what we call "reality."

The realization that all of what which we call solid and real (money, property, reputation, identity, wealth, etc.) does not belong to a world that is fundamentally different from, or more solid than, the artifacts of the "less real" digital world where we encounter bizarre things like blockchains and ledgers, DAOs, DeFis, cryptocurrencies, dApps, gas fees, minting, NFTs, and much more; this realization that we are dealing with an ecosystem of realities that share in common the collective ascent granted by the participants to the world they are sharing – a world where people buy things, cooperate with one another, own objects, transfer wealth, information, affection, display pride, and so forth – enables us to open ourselves up to a whole world of opportunity that would otherwise remain out of reach if we insisted on mystifying the artifacts and the instruments of the digital world (the so-called Web3) and quarantining it to its separate and not equal bizarro world, populated by bizarro people doing bizarro things. In other words, the opportunity in front of us is in pulling these instruments into what we loosely call "the real world" (the world of houses and food and diplomas and cash money), poking at them, and finding out how we can use them to solve real problems. And, as we do this, we come to understand that we can not only solve existing "real" problems but in fact create some real value that we otherwise would not have been able to conceive of, even better.

In this chapter, our aim is twofold: first, to propose a methodology for identifying how this exotic thing called an NFT can be used in the real world to solve real problems, and second, to apply this methodology to explain and surface the value that NFTs are delivering and can deliver in five "real-life" sectors: event ticketing, food and drink, fashion, financial loans, and supply chain management.

The Methodology

Let us reiterate our basic, fundamental insight: the backbone of each of the worlds that we inhabit, whether we want to call such worlds "real," "virtual," "augmented," "mixed," or whatever else, is nothing more and nothing less, for the purposes of inhabiting those worlds, than the respective ontologies of such worlds – ontologies which we, the people who populate and navigate those worlds, have come to accept and use and take very seriously. The additional corollary insight is that these ontologies are sustained by nothing more than our assent, our acceptance of them, and that they, these worlds, would vanish as soon as we decide to no longer take their respective ontologies seriously, should we decide to do so. It is *within* these ontologies that we create our multiple phenomenological *immanences*, or more plainly, our ways of being in each world as we inhabit our multiple identities – our personal habitats – sometimes more than one habitat at a time.

The innovation here, if we can call it one, as we attempt to identify value opportunities that the ontology attached to the world NFTs introduces in "*a* real world" (for there are *many* real worlds) is to flesh out to whatever extent we can a given "real-world" ontology and mash it up with the NFT ontology and then see what we can obtain. More specifically, the project at hand is to identify those problems that exist in the ontology of a chosen "real world" that can be solved with the introduction of an NFT ontology (for there, also, thanks to smart contracts, there exists a multiplicity of them), now that the objects of the two ontologies coexist in a mashed-up ontology, with proviso, obviously, that this newly mashed-up ontology is taken seriously by those humans that live in and through it. Beyond identifying problems to solve, the hope is that we will also be able to identify *opportunities* for delivering value that is enabled by the new mashed-up ontology, given for, as almost always, a mash-up is always greater than the sum of the parts that were mashed up together.

Applications and Use Cases

The best way to explain what we mean by all of this is to go through the four "real worlds" that we have chosen – events, food and drink, fashion, and supply chain management – one by one, and apply our methodology against each one.

Events

This is the world of, among other things, tickets, ticket issuers, performers, event organizers, event suppliers, advertisers, festivals, passes, authorized ticket sellers, scalpers, fans of the performers, members of the media, venues, and event-goers.

In this world, (1) fans buy tickets from authorized ticket sellers, or, if they can't find tickets from such authorized sellers, they buy them from scalpers, who sell them at a higher price than the ticket was initially selling for; (2) fans attend events, miss them because something came up at the last minute, and attend them but are not happy with them; (3) performers of an event perform and receive compensation for their work, with which they may or may not be happy, and engage with fans, who may respond to their performance in fulfilling ways or dispiriting ways; (4) organizers of these events set up the events, find advertisers, engage with suppliers, provide security to these events, engage the media, with the authorities, if such engagements are necessary, etc.

With this quick run-through of our rather simplified ontology of the world of events, we can already identify several of the chronic problems that the world of events is plagued with. Here is a small list of them:

1. Fake tickets

2. Ticket scalping and opportunistic middlemen

3. Lost tickets

4. Canceled events

5. Unhappy fans that go unidentified, with little chance to make up for their disappointment

6. Very happy fans that go unidentified, with little chance of leveraging their happiness

NFTs can potentially help solve many of these problems in the following ways:

1. Every ticket is an NFT, and hence, the ticket's provenance is public and immutable. And so, in one fell swoop, fake tickets disappear from the landscape.

2. Every ticket is an NFT, and hence, in the NFT's smart contract, a clause can be introduced that would prohibit the owner of the NFT from selling it. And in one fell swoop, the scalper disappears from the landscape.

3. If the ticket you are holding in your digital wallet is an NFT, then, as long as you don't lose your digital wallet, your ticket is safe and you will never need to look for it.

4. An event is canceled and anyone who bought a ticket for the canceled event can either choose to accept a refund or register for an event in the future. With NFTs, the effort of making this possible is not more than a few lines of programming or the triggering for some rules in some software stack. For both the organizers and the ticket holders, all of this happens by magic, with no more than clicking a button or two on an interface from them.

5. You are an artist and you owe your livelihood to the fans. Without them, you can't put food on the table, let alone practice your art, your craft, or deliver your wisdom. Ensuring that you are aware of what your fans feel about you, and that you engage with those who were not happy to regain their enthusiastic

support, is something that you would probably wish you could do. Without NFTs that can easily track who attended which event, and that can easily enable the attendees to share their experiences, making it up to disappointed fans is almost impossible. With NFTs, this all becomes, again, a matter of an app or a web interface.

6. The same holds with fans who are very happy with the event: such fans would be ripe for buying merchandise, for spreading the word, for promoting the performer's brand, the venue, and the organizers, and for buying tickets for future events. Again, all of this is nearly impossible to do without NFTs, but more than possible, in fact, easy to do with NFTs.

An Example of a Current Implementation

As of this time of writing, the most promising companies in the NFT space are indeed those that promise to have a real-life impact by solving real problems, companies that enable event hosting and e-ticketing, among other adjacent services, with the blockchain and smart contract as part of their tech infrastructure. Examples of such companies are EventsFrame, GUTS, UTIX, Blocktix, Plentix, and TicketMint to single out just a small subset of such companies.

Food and Drink

This is the world of, among other things, reservations, tables, hosts, fancy meals, sandwiches, deserts, coffee, wine, wine bottles, patrons, restaurants, chefs, recipes, ingredients, and cocktails,

In this world, (1) restaurant reservations are made and canceled; (2) restaurant meals are eaten, and patrons are happy or unhappy with the meal; (3) patrons are in the restaurant for the couple of hours or so, and they are either happy or unhappy with the service provided by the host, or the condition of the restaurant (too hot or too cold or shabbily decorated), or the location of their table; (4) outside of the restaurant setting, people buy bottles of wine, and some of them are very intentional buyers and seek out high-quality wine for which they are willing to pay a high price; (5) outside of the restaurant setting, people cook at home, and many are always on the hunt for killer recipes from chefs that they follow (perhaps the chef at their favorite restaurant).

Again, after this quick run-through of our rather simplified ontology of the world of food and drink, here are several of the chronic problems that one encounters in the world of food and drink. Here is a small list of them:

1. Last-minute cancellations or no-shows (a big problem for the restaurant)

2. Bad food (for the patron)

3. Bad service (for the patron)

4. Inauthentic wine

5. Unhappy patrons that go unidentified, with little chance to make up for their disappointment

6. Very happy patrons that go unidentified, with little chance of leveraging their happiness

NFTs can help solve many of these problems, and even open new opportunities, in the following ways:

1. If every reservation is an NFT, in the NFT's smart contract, a clause can be introduced that would charge a fee for any cancellations or no-shows. Additionally, if someone with a long track record of canceling tried to make a reservation, the smart contract can be written in such a way that such a person's reservation is rejected.

2. In cases where the patron is not happy with
    the service or the food, if the establishment is
    itself an NFT, software can be written to enable
    only those who actually made reservations (the
    reservations themselves NFTs on the ledgers)
    and ate at the restaurant (they were checked
    in to the establishment), to put in a review on
    their experience. This would enable an almost
    hermetically honest rating of the restaurant
    (something that plagues services such as Yelp!,
    where fake reviews in both directions create
    distorted evaluations).

3. Similarly for those who were happy, here, the
    opportunity is to leverage such happy customers
    for spreading the word, enrolling them into loyalty
    programs, offering them discounts, and including
    them in exclusive events (e.g., Thanksgiving, New
    Year's Eve, Valentine's Day).

4. Imagine every physical bottle of wine is paired with
    an NFT that contains with its metadata important
    details about the bottle of wine, such as its vintage,
    vineyard, region, and any other distinguishing
    characteristics, then attach a physical identifier to
    the bottle itself (for instance, unique QR code). In
    this way, to authenticate the bottle, a user can scan
    or verify the physical identifier, which will provide
    access to the NFT's metadata, which could then be
    compared to the bottle, and its authenticity either
    established or rejected. Compare this to what one
    need to do today: which simply to trust the seller, or
    to hire an expensive connoisseurs who will look at

several details, such as the print type of the labels, the age of the paper, ink and font, print methods, aging techniques – in other words, someone who is probably very expensive to hire given the deep knowledge that they have had to accumulate.

An Example of a Current Implementation

Bored Breakfast Club is a Web3 NFT coffee subscription company that offers a collection of NFT breakfast scenes living on the Ethereum blockchain. Each NFT is a unique, digital collectible and serves as a membership token unlocking free shipments of freshly roasted coffee. The NFT also provides the buyer with access to an online community, live events, digital content library, and discounts on supplemental bags of coffee.

Fashion

This is the world of, among other things, brands, shoes, clothes, styles, accessories, factories, workers, models, stores, and fashion shows.

In this world, (1) people buy clothes, (2) styles are in fashion during a period of time, (3) styles are out of fashion, (4) styles once out of fashion are back in vogue, (4) brands issue new products, and (5) brands announce that they have discontinued a product.

Here are a handful of potential problems and opportunities that one encounters in the world of fashion:

1. A company is selling clothing that was manufactured in a developing nation under near-slave conditions and a story is breaking out about how the brand manufacturing it has profited greatly from the sales of these products.

2. A limited edition of a product sold by a brand is being bought and resold in the marketplace at a high premium.

3. A sneaker company wants to set up a promotion event by entering into a lottery the first 100 people who bought a specific shoe brand five years ago.

4. Someone wants to buy a highly sought-after limited-edition bag but they are not sure whether or not that bag is authentic.

NFTs can help solve many of these problems, and even open new opportunities, in the following ways:

1. If each clothing item is an NFT that contains metadata about each step of the production, packaging, shipment, and delivery of the product to the retail store, a brand associated with product can track exactly where its products are made, how they are packaged and shipped, and who transports and delivers them. This then would enable whoever in the company is in charge of the brand to quickly identify any risk points that may emerge – for instance, a manufacturer whose workers are kept in near-slave conditions – and quickly to eliminate the risk (for instance, seeking out a new manufacturer who treats their workers much better).

2. To curb the practice of buying a limited-edition product only to resell it for high profit, a brand might require anyone who wishes to buy the product to place an NFT provided by the brand inside the wallet of the buyer, and market the product as one that comes with an NFT that enables buyer to own a virtual badge that they can flash in their Instagram or Twitter or other virtual places. The NFTs can then be attached to smart contracts that forbid the

reselling of the NFT, making the physical product, now that the buyer is not able to buy the associated NFT, far less attractive than it would have been if it came with the NFT.

3. When buying a pair of highly covered sneakers, a buyer may also get an NFT that goes into their digital wallet as proof that they own the coveted pair of sneakers. For the brand, the distributed NFTs could serve as a way to market to the NFT owners in ways that they could not have been able to do without the NFTs, such as identifying the first 100 people who bought the sneakers exactly five years to the day of the sneaker's fifth anniversary.

4. Similar to the bottle of wine example in the previous section, imagine pairing a brand bag with an NFT that contains the bag's metadata, with specific identifying marks on the bag that would be nearly impossible for someone to identify, let alone replicate. Only someone who bought the bag for real would have the specific NFT that contains the unique information on the bag. This would not, of course, make it mathematically impossible for someone to sell fake bags, but it makes such counterfeit goods extremely expensive to produce, at the very least far more expensive than just slapping an easy to replicate brand logo on any old cheap bag.

An Example of a Current Implementation

WrapTag is a service that provides physical near-field communication tags which contain a WrapTag NFT verifying the authenticity, ownership, and history of the item. In other words, it is a solution that twins a physical thing with a record of that thing on the blockchain and blocks attempts to assert ownership of fake items.

Supply Chain

Here, we are dealing with the world of, among other things, shipments, pallets, warehouses, demand, permits, shelf lives, suppliers, transportation, last miles, and labor.

In this world, (1) factories make products, (2) truckers drive trucks to transport goods to shipment points, (3) permits are issued to enable ships to dock into ports or leave ports with pallets of products, (4) received product are stored in warehouses, and (5) customers buy things by going to stores or an online through ecommerce websites.

Here are a handful of potential problems and opportunities that one encounters in the logistics and supply chain world:

1.   Truckers quit their jobs.

2.   A factory has slowed down production because of missing parts.

3.   Products with a rapidly approaching expiration date are languishing in a warehouse because the paperwork needed to transport the products is missing due to a shortage in the staffing of permit issuing authority.

4.   Demand for a product is slowing down because of economic conditions.

5.   On April 24, 2013, a building Rana Plaza in Savar, a suburb of Dhaka, Bangladesh, that housed several garment factories, a bank, and shops collapsed, resulting in the loss of over 1,100 lives and left more

than 2,500 people injured. The catastrophe was
one of the deadliest industrial disasters in history.
Most of the victims were factory workers, primarily
women, who were producing clothing for major
global brands, such as H&M, Gucci, and Versace.
Brands claimed that they were not aware that their
clothes were being made in such appalling work
conditions. They blamed lower-tier managers,
their sourcing partners, and the local and national
governments in Bangladesh.

Here is how NFTs can help:

1. Imagine each trucker and each truck have each
    an NFT associated with them, and that up-to-date
    metadata is kept on each trucker and each truck,
    enabling management to know exactly the most
    minute fluctuations in the supply of truckers and
    trucks and where and when bottlenecks are starting
    to build before they build and become manifest,
    creating last-minute pressures on truckers to drive
    long hours to make up for the shortages resulting
    from the bubbling shortages. Such information
    could help not only the private companies but
    the local, state, and federal government engage in
    actions where they are able to, to assist in averting
    the buildup of transportation bottlenecks that
    may result in shortages of critical products such as
    medicine, medical equipment, and baby formula,
    as we saw happen during and after the COVID
    pandemic. Software written on top of the NFTs, in
    combination with AI that can detect patterns and
    make predictions given prior scenarios, can provide

actionable information much earlier in time, when quick adjustments, potentially themselves recommended by the AI, can be made.

2.   Imagine each factory is an NFT whose metadata – such as production volume and staffing levels – are available publicly in times of crisis, enabling everyone in the ecosystem that is vested in the smooth running of the factory as well as those who make critical decisions, such purchasing, stocking, and staffing, of their respective organizations, to act accordingly. Being able to obtain such data in a reliable way and in a timely basis can be the difference between an averted economic crisis and a cascading one that touches many critical sectors of the economy.

3.   NFTs can also help ensure that information about products with short shelf lives and expiration dates is available reliably and in real time to ensure proper prioritization of resource allocation, including staffing, and timely communication and coordination with various stakeholders, including government authorities to expedite procedures that otherwise would result expensive delays and general population negative impacts.

4.   The journey of a product usually begins six to twelve months before it is finally sold, whether through a retail or a wholesale channel. Given that nearly every service in the supply delivery chain is outsourced to some third party, that may itself further subcontract the service to a fourth party

down the line, tracking the source of any product, let alone a product component, let alone the path of its journey, is almost physically impossible to do. Twinning products, and even parts of products, with NFTs, would make such tracking almost trivial. No more islands of systems and record-keeping protocols that don't speak to each other, or can't talk to each other because integrations between the systems don't exist. There is one protocol, the NFT, and one system, the blockchain, that everyone is using to refer to the product or its part, and to track what happens to that product or its parts along the way.

5. Imagine if we could tell, with the simple scan of a tag on a clothing item, exactly where each item was made, where it originated, how it was transported, where it was housed, and so forth. Brands would no longer be able to plead ignorance, as they did in the case of the Rana Plaza in 2013. Nor would reporters and their editors in media outlets, who are supposed to be working on stories of exploitation, can claim that it is expensive to report on such stories.

An Example of a Current Implementation

Nestlé, a global food and beverage company, launched Chain of Origin to provide supply chain transparency "from crop to cup" for coffee beans, making all record of all transactions throughout the supply chain transparent, immutable, and verifiable. This enables Nestlé's partners to interact in a trustworthy and efficient manner. This solution also makes possible the spotting of any mistakes, malpractices, or tampering, for quick reaction.

Summary

As things stand today, in 2023, no more than one out of four people in the United States has even heard of the abbreviation "NFT," while the majority of those who have heard it do not fully understand it, or understand it only as something related to digital artifacts such as images, videos, and audio files. In this understanding of NFTs, there is the real world where real things affect people in real ways, and then there is the world of NFTs, a world of make-believe, pretending, and hype, a game of sorts that people who are interested in that game play and take seriously. Such a conception of NFTs is deeply misguided, and in its misguidance misses a whole world of opportunities. Our real world is no more real and no more tangible than the digital world: in both worlds we deal with concepts and categories, conventions and protocols, and what holds everything together in both worlds in assent of those who are participating and acting in this world. Once we realize that the real world and the digital world can be merged into one world of coexisting objects, possibilities for innovative ways of not only solving problems but creating new value quickly emerge. As things, we have barely even begun to scratch the surface of what is possible. Exciting solutions and innovations are ahead of us.

CHAPTER 8

The Future of NFTs

The future of NFTs is intimately intertwined with the future of the Web. NFTs did not emerge ex nihilo, nor were they the accidental exotic creations of geeks experimenting in their secluded dark-screened labs. NFTs emerged to solve a long-standing problem in the digital world, that of non-scarcity, and along the way revealed that they could deliver much more than a simulation "real life" by introducing commodity constraints so that we may re-create the basic building blocks of our real world, brick-and-mortar economies in the digital world. NFTs, we discovered, could in fact help us deliver on that original vision that came to life with the emergence of the Web back in the early 1990s, a web that was distributed, democratic, open, accessible to all, and safe and secure. As things stand today, 30 years on, we remain very far from that dream place where we wanted to go.

A Tale of Three Webs

The pursuit of that dream came to a sudden halt, it seemed, with the stock market crash of March 2000, a crash that washed off all that "silliness" and "insanity," we were told, that had been bubbling and brewing as our imaginations shot off to new exhilarating heights and depths. The party was over, it was announced, no more "irrational exuberance," and the clearing at once commenced, sweeping the debris of that decade-long experiment off into some unmarked dustbin to make way for the next phase: the "sober," "subdued," and "orderly" Web.

© Ahmed Bouzid, Paolo Narciso, and Steve Wood 2023
A. Bouzid et al., *NFTs for Business*, https://doi.org/10.1007/978-1-4842-9777-3_8

135

Not all was lost, we were assured, however. The pipes underneath remained, along with the various infrastructures and the learnings and the experiments and the failures from that zany, crazy, wacky decade of the 1990s; pipes that made possible all that we now take for granted – from smartphones to videos to smart speakers to AirPods to the podcasts that we can't sleep without.

Many like us, those who actively participated in that wonderful madness, are experiencing a visceral sense of *deja vu* with NFTs and other emerging Web3 tools. Wild claims and naysayers, thrilling prospects and dark counter-visions, heady dreams and the scoffing of realists – none of that is really news. But instead of the brick-and-mortar baseline of the mid-1990s, our current baseline is our mature Web 2.0-infused lifeworld, one that has long figured out how one can make lots and lots of money from it. But more than making money, how we live our daily life and how we exist as sentient humans. Being "off the grid" is now such an odd state that one needs to announce it to others days if not weeks in advance. And even then, we are never off the grid.

Hence the challenge: while the deltas between going from no-Web to Web 1.0 or from Web 1.0 to Web 2.0 are significant, even obvious and relatively easy to grasp, going from Web 2.0 to Web 3.0 is apparently not.

But a brief pause to quickly define what the three iterations of the Web mean in general terms.

Web 1.0 can be described as the state of the Web when the vast majority of those who surfed it were passive readers, while a very tiny number were creators of that content. The mission of Web1 was to enable those who had the means (usually universities) to create content, and those who had the means to look for such content (Yahoo, AltaVista) and find it using an interface that did not require any knowledge other than clicking on links and perhaps (in rare occasions) filling out forms (Mosaic, Netscape).

With **Web 2.0,** we went from a few passive readers looking for and reading documents, and fewer creators of such content, to a much larger number not only of readers but creators. Publishing blogs and websites by the intrepid (Blogger) were the first Web2 actions, along with curating content, podcasting, and social media. It is during this phase that application programming interfaces and the protocols that support them were born (REST, RPC, SOAP, XML, JSON, etc.).

The jumps from no-Web to Web 1.0 to Web 2.0 are therefore easy enough to grasp – at least in hindsight. We went from a very tiny minority creating and sharing information to a full-on democratization and mainstreaming of creation and distribution. The purported nonlinear jump from Web 2.0 to Web 3.0, however, is apparently harder to characterize.

Or is it? Because, we all know that it's very easy to see phases and milestones when one looks back. At the time, when we were in the middle of "evolving," the Web was a newfangled thing, and the vast majority of people did not take it seriously, let alone see it for the seismic shift that it has turned out to be. This included Bill Gates, who published his 1995 book, *The Road Ahead*, without mentioning the Web at all, only to quickly fix the blunderous miss by tacking on a chapter on the Web in a hurried second edition.

Did we predict that we would order almost all of our stuff using the Web, that we would bank using the Web, that we would communicate with each other using the Web, that we would self-medicate using the Web, that we would learn using the Web, that we would find the solution to any of our problems? This includes how to extract a broken key by watching a YouTube video that someone posted – who knows why? In essence, live online?

No, we didn't. Not at all.

But the fact is that the future was already there, like the future is always here, except that, as William Gibson's famous saying goes, "it's just not evenly distributed" – yet.

I suspect that the same is taking place today.

To begin understanding what Web 3.0 is all about, digging into the technologies that purport to implement it – blockchains, NFTs, DAOs, DeFi, etc. – I discovered, is the wrong way to go about reaching such understanding. Doing so would be akin to diving into TCP/IP, HTTP, FTP, SMTP, or XML, to understand what Web1 or Web2 were all about. Instead, a more fruitful way perhaps is to enumerate the values, the principles, and the goals of this coming phase, as well as the problems that we wish this new iteration to solve for us.

In a nutshell, here is what I have come to understand what Web 3.0 to be about after engaging via phone and Zoom conversations, and email exchanges with more than two dozen Web 3.0 experts and practitioners. Among other things, Web 3.0 is about decentralization, frictionless transaction, collective and community base creation, ownership, access to meaning rather than simply to information, creation of meaning rather than just information, and security and privacy.

Back to the Future

What was surprising to me about the Web 3.0 experts and practitioners that we spoke with is how allergic they all were to speaking in inflated terms. My surprise is clearly a reflection of the overall skeptical Zeitgeist over the whole Web 3.0 project, absorbed even by someone like me who comes to Web 3.0 with a sympathetic disposition.

"Folks are turned off by the hype and the noise," Shannon Wu, co-founder at Identity Review, told me in a Zoom interview. "But when I share a lot of the stories of what it was like years ago when the very earliest Web3 companies were starting," she added, "I think they see a lot of parallels with when the Internet first started around individual rights, scalability, privacy, thinking about user rights."

Olivia Baker, tech editor and director of Web3 Innovation Fellowship, also at Identity Review, noted on her part that, "if you peel away the muck and you really give [people] facts... it's actually quite easy to use that specific evidence to convince them... that there is actually validity in this particular way to look at systems." This, she noted, works "even within a university environment where a lot of people... are inherently skeptical of things like blockchain, Web3, all these concepts that sound very nebulous at first..."

Asked what they thought about William Gibson's famous saying about the future already being here with us now in the context of Web3, several experts that I spoke with agreed and provided some insightful and interesting examples and observations.

Drew Riester, blockchain engineer at ARRIVANT, made the wonderfully surprising observation that we are witnessing the emergence of "a separation of Money and State" and added that if successful, such a separation might "be as important as the separation of Church and State that Martin Luther began in 1512."

Manuel Urrego, head of product at Viker, pointed to the NFL's Green Bay Packers, the only sports team that is owned by their fans. David Shuttleworth, DeFi economist at Consensys, agreed and noted that the Packers example "represents the potential of fractionalized ownership, which could be achieved through an NFT system."

But it was Zenobia Godschalk, founder of ZAG Communications and SVP at Swirlds Labs, whose mission is to drive adoption of the Hedera distributed public ledger for decentralized applications, who brought things home to me by pointing to what I have always believed to be nothing short of a miracle in the shining hills of the Web landscape: Wikipedia.

Here we have a website whose content is created by everyone but owned by no one, where no central overseer runs the show, and where value is delivered for free and for everybody. How such a marvel could have been imagined in the first place, let alone built, sustained, and nurtured for so long to a thriving ecosystem for over two decades (we now have not just Wikipedia but Wikimedia) has always struck me as something almost inexplicable in our deeply capitalistic society and economy, where, if you can't monetize it, it will die.

And yet, I must confess that I have not donated once to this marvel that I have admired since the very first time I started using it in early 2001, even when I am asked to donate. Shame on me. Can Web3 help me be more true to my values?

"Every time you go to Wikipedia there's the banner across the top where they are begging you for money," Godschalk said to my vigorous nods of agreement, and added: "If you apply the Web3 elements and you can say, 'Great, now I can pay a micropayment every time I read an article,' and that helps support the distributed infrastructure that runs Wikipedia...."

Brady Gentile, also at Swirlds Labs as director of marketing and Web3 ecosystems strategy, pointed to another miracle of the Web: open source. "Open source has always existed," he noted when we spoke, "and a lot of the open source software is incorporated in the operating systems and the applications that [we] use today."

But, he added, "historically, it has been incredibly difficult to create a business around open source models. Most of the successful ones have to [use a] services model, and Red Hat was probably one of the very few open source companies. Today, you have open source and it is ubiquitous in Web3 – it's a layer 1 network, Defi protocol, an exchange, a marketplace.... The difference is now we have the ability to have assets that are associated with those open source projects, so a contributor has the incentive because they are passionate about building and contributing to those open source projects, but additionally, there is an incentive model for them where typically they are token holders of the token associated with that project and as they build and as they create value for it."

Ian Brent, Web3 growth manager at UppticWeb3, shared with me a really good example to explain in terms that everyone can understand the otherwise mystifying concept of the "immutable blockchain" and what it means for someone to follow every transaction that, say, an NFT may have undergone: Google Docs! "You collaborate with all of your teammates and can review any and all revisions for a complete historical record of ins and outs of the sheet."

Other examples cited by the Web 3.0 experts and practitioners that I engaged include the following:

1. Online payments: Certainly not decentralized, but we are now able to move at the speed of the digital: I can pay using PayPal or enter my credit card safely, and have my account activated immediately.

2. Generative AI and chatbots: These would stand for the beginning of the Semantic Web. I can now ask questions such as "Why were Corn Flakes invented?" or "Is it safe to eat wild onions?" and get back pithy answers rather than documents to wade through.

3. Signal, Telegram: These enable me to communicate securely.

4. Paywalls: Paying for the value that I want to consume (*The Washington Post*, *The New York Times*, Spotify, Netflix) rather than selling my information via Ads.

Of course, none of these examples, as currently served, fully realizes all, or even most, of the aspirations of Web3 in its full glory. They are all still resting on the Web2 stack whose underlying architecture (servers, private centers of power, egregious power consumption) are clearly not adequate to deliver what we want more of, and do so on a scalable and sustainable basis.

Nevertheless, the promise itself of Web3 is something thrilling and exhilarating and clearly delineates the outlines of a horizon that we wish to move toward. But, as Raunak Singh, blockchain engineer at Mimo, noted: "I agree with the William Gibson quote, but I think the reason why the future is not evenly distributed is that the newly developed tech solves some problems much better than others."

Cryptocurrency, which is the one Web3 technology that has penetrated the mainstream's consciousness the most deeply, is undoubtedly here to stay. Even up-to-now-stalwart detractors of the technology are starting to soften, while tech giants, whom one might imagine may be demurring over the emergence of a far more decentralized tech ecosystem than we have been used to for the last two decades, are embracing Web3.

As Bertrand Portier, principal at Google Cloud Web3 and Digital Assets, wrote me in answer to the question I had sent him about what, in his own words, is the promise of Web3: "The promise of Web3 is a decentralized and transparent world that allows individuals and organizations to prosper by taking control of their digital assets and attributes."

But beyond mainstreaming crypto, another technology that is surely here to stay with us is smart contracts.

"While inherently complex," observed David Shuttleworth of Consensys, "even at a very fundamental level the prospect of direct, peer-to-peer interactions that are publicly auditable, fully transparent, and which remove the need for a third-party, is a tremendously attractive proposition. And this is exactly what smart contracts achieve."

Beyond the Hype

As things stand, the blockchains and the cryptocurrencies on top of them, the CeFi and the DeFi stacks, and the dApp and DAO platforms, along with their smart contracts and their NFTs, are all in a state of rickety imperfection, full of gaping holes and at times nearly absurd irrationality (how can one really talk about breaking free from a centralized paradigm when one hosts their NFTs under the banner of an OpenSea or a Rarible, both no less central and controlled than any marketplace that braces the current Web landscape?). But something clearly is happening – something that I have no doubt is both wonderful and at the same time dangerous.

Art and Collectibles

NFTs have already shown us how profound of an impact this technology can have on the art world. NFTs enable artists to tokenize their digital creations and sell them directly to those who are interested in their art and wish to collect it. As long as there are artists willing to create and who wish to make money from their art, and as long as there are buyers who believe in the artists that they follow, trends will continue. The pudding is real, and as long as embracing NFTs enables artists to bypass traditional intermediaries, to monetize their work, and to gain greater control over their intellectual property, NFTs will grow in presence and will go mainstream in due time.

Music and Entertainment

The music industry has similarly been witnessing the growing benefits of NFTs, with musicians now able to tokenize not only their songs and their albums, but also issue limited-edition releases by minting a limited number of NFTs representing special editions of their albums, EPs, and singles. Often, such NFTs include bonus tracks and behind-the-scenes content.

Gaming and Virtual Worlds

NFTs have already gained significant traction in the gaming industry with the tokenization of virtual items and in-game assets. This trend is likely to intensify, as NFTs enable real, verifiable ownership and the transferability of digital items across multiple gaming platforms.

Moreover, the integration of blockchain technology with both virtual reality and augmented reality experiences is expected to create immersive experiences where NFTs play an important role.

Fractional Ownership and Liquidity

Beyond direct, verifiable ownership, NFTs can enable fractional ownership, allowing multiple individuals to own a fraction of some high-value digital asset. This enables the democratization of access to expensive items, such as rare collectibles and expensive virtual real estate. Moreover, by enabling seamless trading and instantaneous transfers, NFTs enhance liquidity, thereby unlocking new possibilities for investment and economic participation.

Digital Identity and Personal Branding

NFTs have started to play a crucial role in establishing and authenticating digital identities. Thanks to their tokenization, unique digital assets can now act as verifiable proof of ownership, expertise, and accomplishments. A compelling example is social tokenization: the use of NFTs in conjunction with social tokens, which are tokens representing a person's community or social capital. Such tokens allow individuals, for instance, to reward their supporters or fans directly. By combining NFTs with social tokens, individuals can offer members of their community of supporters unique benefits, access to exclusive communities, or voting rights on certain decisions, strengthening personal branding and cultivating a loyal following.

Challenges and Potential Solutions

But the road ahead remains full of challenges and the rate of adoption of NFTs will depend on how fast these challenges are overcome. Here are the main challenges ahead.

Lack of Awareness and Education

As of this time of writing, the basic reality remains that the vast majority of potential users and creators remain unaware of what NFTs are and how they can be utilized. To the extent that most people are aware of NFTs, they have come to equate them with vaporware crypto scams. Critical to the adoption of NFTs is the education of individuals about what NFTs are and, crucially, the concrete benefits that they yield, the real problems that they solve, along with a sober enumeration of the potential risks associated with NFTs.

Trust and Verification

Verifying the originality and ownership of NFTs can be challenging, especially when it comes to digital art and collectibles. Since authenticity and provenance are vital in the world of digital assets, developing standardized verification processes, reputation systems, and blockchain-based provenance records will take us a long way toward building trust and enhancing the credibility of NFTs.

Market Speculation and Volatility

The rapid rise of NFTs in the last few years has attracted speculative investors, leading to inflated prices that are clearly detached from the underlying value of the digital assets. The fact that NFTs of nothing more than an image can sell for tens of millions of dollars coupled with a near lack of understanding of what NFTs are and how they work understandably creates suspicion of manipulation, if not outright foul play. This in turn has unsurprisingly deterred both creators and buyers from participating in the NFT market. Therefore, essential to sustainable growth is the establishment of market stability, responsible investment practices, and mechanisms to determine the true value of NFTs.

Technical Complexity

NFTs operate on blockchain technology, which can easily be challenging for nontechnical users to understand and navigate. Currently, the process of creating, buying, and selling NFTs often involves, among other actions, interacting with cryptocurrency wallets, decentralized exchanges, and blockchain networks. Crucial to overcoming the technology barrier is to simplify the user experience by creating user-friendly platforms that anyone can use.

Scalability and Network Congestion

Blockchain networks, especially those utilizing proof-of-work consensus algorithms like Ethereum, continue to face scalability issues. High transaction fees and network congestion can create barriers for NFT adoption, particularly for lower-value transactions or frequent trading. Unless and until the minting, buying, and selling of NFTs is scalable, the NFT market will remain a niche interest. Potential solutions include (1) exploring alternative consensus mechanisms, such as proof of stake, which consume significantly less energy and can process transactions more efficiently compared to proof-of-work networks; (2) adopting layer-two solutions and the development of more scalable blockchains; and

(3) establishing interoperability protocols, such as Polkadot and Cosmos, to enable seamless communication and asset transfer between different blockchain networks. These solutions facilitate the movement of NFTs across multiple chains, reducing congestion on any single network.

Copyright and Intellectual Property Challenges

As promising as they are for helping creators protect and benefit from their work, NFTs do however present us with several complex legal and intellectual property issues. The digital nature of NFTs and the ease of replicating digital assets raise concerns about copyright infringement and ownership disputes. Essential to providing the necessary protections and to ensure fair compensation will be the development of robust legal frameworks, decentralized copyright registries, and transparent licensing mechanisms.

Environmental Concerns

Proof-of-work blockchains, such as Ethereum, require significant computational power and electricity consumption for the mining and validation of transactions, resulting in substantial carbon emissions. Shifting from energy-intensive proof-of-work consensus mechanisms to more environmentally friendly alternatives like proof of stake is one obvious step toward significantly reducing the carbon footprint of NFT transactions. Also important would be the introduction of regulations that require NFT platforms to disclose the energy usage of their operations, and creators to provide details about the energy consumption involved in the creation and minting of NFTs. Vital also would be the establishment of close collaboration among NFT platforms, creators, environmental organizations, and researchers to invest in research and development that explore innovative solutions, such as green mining technologies, energy-efficient consensus algorithms, or sustainable blockchain infrastructure.

Summary

NFTs are a solution to the long-standing problem of digital non-scarcity, offering the potential to re-create real-world economic concepts in the digital realm. The chapter outlines the progression from the early days of the Web (Web 1.0) to the democratized and interactive landscape of Web 2.0, leading to the emergence of Web 3.0 and its defining values: decentralization, frictionless transactions, collective creation, ownership, access to meaning, and security/privacy. We discuss the challenges of grasping the leap from Web 2.0 to Web 3.0 and drawing parallels to historical transitions in web development. Notable aspects of Web 3.0, including decentralization, transparency, and the potential for new economic models, are explored through conversations with experts. The chapter addresses the adoption of NFTs in diverse sectors like art, music, gaming, and personal branding while also acknowledging challenges such as lack of awareness, trust issues, market speculation, technical complexity, scalability, copyright concerns, and environmental impact. Despite the challenges, the author expresses optimism about the transformative potential of NFTs within the broader context of the evolving web landscape.

CHAPTER 9

Uncovering Trends and Other Applications of NFTS

As we stand on the precipice of a new era, the digital age continues to redefine our lives in ways that were once beyond imagination. One revolutionary concept that has rapidly entered mainstream consciousness is that of non-fungible tokens, or NFTs.

As we've defined in this book, an NFT is simply a type of digital asset that represents real-world objects like art, music, in-game items, and videos. By now, you should think of it as a unique certificate of ownership for digital creations, all secured with the same technology that powers cryptocurrencies like Bitcoin and Ethereum – blockchain. This technology ensures that the ownership of these digital assets is transparent, secure, and most importantly, unchangeable.

We've journeyed together through the fascinating world of NFTs, understanding their impact, their potential, and the changes they've brought about. We've seen how artists are now able to directly reach their audiences, how creators are empowered, and how collectors can own a unique piece of digital property.

© Ahmed Bouzid, Paolo Narciso, and Steve Wood 2023
A. Bouzid et al., *NFTs for Business*, https://doi.org/10.1007/978-1-4842-9777-3_9

But as we delve into this final chapter of our exploration, we must gaze into the horizon and ponder – what's next for NFTs? As any strategist will tell you, the key to understanding the future lies in recognizing emerging trends and applications. Just like surfers, we must spot the waves before they form and understand where they are likely to crash. And that's precisely what this chapter aims to do.

We'll dive into how NFTs might redefine the future of intellectual property rights, and even examine their potential in something as tangible as real estate. We'll also navigate the exciting intersection of NFTs and decentralized finance, discuss the challenges that might arise, and highlight what you, as an engaged reader, should watch out for.

Buckle up as we journey into the heart of the digital revolution. The future is unwritten, and NFTs hold a powerful pen. Welcome to our concluding chapter – a glimpse into the untapped potential and exciting future of NFTs.

NFTs and the Future of Intellectual Property Rights

NFTs have been quietly working their magic on intellectual property (IP) rights. As we look into the future, their impact becomes increasingly profound and far-reaching.

As we've previously explored, music artists are quickly embracing NFTs as a way to monetize their work in a direct and efficient way. Picture a world where artists release their music as NFTs, allowing fans not just to listen, but to "own" a unique piece of their favorite song, album artwork, or even a live concert experience. In this realm, music fans morph into art collectors, and artists receive fair compensation, free from the constraints of traditional music distribution platforms. In this melodious future, NFTs could bring harmony to the often discordant relationship between artists and the music industry.

Now, let's dim the lights and turn our attention to the world of film. Imagine owning a one-of-a-kind clip from your favorite movie, a special director's cut, or even a unique digital poster. NFTs make this possible, creating a whole new market for film memorabilia and disrupting traditional distribution and licensing. Beyond just ownership, NFTs could also give fans a stake in the film's success, essentially crowdfunded cinema. As the reels of the film industry continue to roll, NFTs promise an interactive and immersive future for cinephiles.

The gaming sector, a digital native, has been quick to adopt and adapt to NFTs. Video games and NFTs are a match made in the virtual heavens. Imagine earning unique digital items during gameplay and trading them in an open marketplace as NFTs. Imagine owning digital real estate in your favorite gaming universe, or even buying and selling characters. In-game economies will transform, and the line between the virtual and real world will blur. NFTs could redefine gaming, making it not just an entertainment source but a potential wealth generator.

And it doesn't stop there. NFTs are poised to make a profound impact on nonprofit organizations as well. Imagine making a charitable donation and receiving an NFT in return as a symbol of your contribution. This NFT could grow in value over time, both as a financial asset and as a token of social impact. In this way, NFTs can facilitate a new era of "impact investing," where doing good is not only emotionally rewarding but also potentially financially beneficial.

A prime example of NFTs being utilized in the nonprofit world is the unique initiative by UNICEF. In 2021, UNICEF launched a program called "The Kids Ethereum Project," which is aimed at supporting Internet connectivity in schools across the globe. As part of this project, UNICEF started to sell "Connectivity" NFTs that represent the impact of the donation.

For instance, if a donor contributes enough to provide Internet connectivity for a school for a month, they receive an NFT representing that contribution. Each of these NFTs is unique and quantifies the impact of the donor's contribution in a tangible way.

Moreover, the NFTs aren't merely digital badges but are pieces of digital art in themselves, created by renowned artists. This not only makes the act of donating more engaging and rewarding but also introduces philanthropists to the world of digital art, thereby expanding the market. The funds raised from the sale of these NFTs are used to finance UNICEF's projects.

What this shows is that NFTs can indeed add a fresh and innovative dimension to charitable giving. By turning donations into unique pieces of art, UNICEF has successfully gamified philanthropy, making it more engaging and rewarding for the donors. This is a great example of how NFTs can revolutionize nonprofits, and it's just the beginning.

The potential of NFTs in the world of intellectual property seems limitless. It's a dynamic, revolutionary force that's reshaping our understanding of ownership, value, and community engagement across industries. As always, the key lies in staying informed, open, and ready for change. Because one thing is clear: the future of NFTs is as exciting and vibrant as the digital art they so often represent.

NFTs in Real Estate and Physical Assets

In the realm of bricks and mortar, the concept of NFTs may seem a little out of place at first glance. However, the beauty of NFTs lies in their ability to bridge the physical and digital worlds. As we continue to unlock the potential of this unique technology, we're starting to see promising applications in sectors as grounded and tangible as real estate.

Picture the idea of "tokenizing" real-world properties. In simpler terms, this means turning a physical asset into a digital token, or NFT, that represents ownership of that asset. Imagine owning an NFT that represents a charming apartment in Paris, a luxurious beachfront property in Malibu, or even a piece of commercial real estate in Manhattan. You might be sitting miles away, but through the power of NFTs, you'd have verifiable ownership of these properties.

Tokenizing real estate could democratize the property market, making it accessible to a wider array of investors. Today, buying a property is a substantial financial commitment, often beyond the reach of many. However, what if a property was divided into numerous NFTs? You could own a fraction of a property, much like owning a share in a company, making real estate investment possible for many who were previously excluded.

Furthermore, NFTs could streamline the often complex process of buying and selling real estate. Smart contracts – self-executing contracts with the agreement directly written into lines of code – could automate the process of property transfers, minimizing bureaucracy and reducing the chances of fraud.

The idea of tokenizing physical assets extends beyond just real estate. It could apply to other tangible commodities such as cars, precious stones, or artwork, creating a link between physical goods and the digital blockchain. This could ensure proof of authenticity and ownership, bringing transparency and security to markets often plagued by counterfeits and fraud.

Looking toward the horizon, the potential for tokenizing real-world assets through NFTs is immense. While there are hurdles to overcome, the promise of a more accessible, transparent, and efficient marketplace is an exciting prospect. In this new world order, owning a piece of the Eiffel Tower or a rare Picasso painting could be just a few clicks away.

However, it's important to note that this application of NFTs isn't without its challenges. Real-world assets, unlike purely digital ones, have a physical presence and are subject to laws and regulations of the jurisdiction they're in. Ensuring that an NFT's ownership accurately reflects these legal rights will be crucial.

NFTs and Decentralized Finance (DeFi)

Imagine a world where financial transactions, loans, trades, and investments all happen without the need for a traditional bank or financial institution. This is the revolutionary world of decentralized finance, or DeFi. It's a system where financial products become available on a public decentralized blockchain network, making them open to anyone to use, rather than going through middlemen like banks or brokers. Now, let's bring NFTs into this mix. The combination sounds intriguing, doesn't it? It's like adding a dash of color to an already vibrant canvas.

So far, NFTs and DeFi have mostly existed as parallel developments within the broader blockchain ecosystem. However, we're beginning to see these worlds converge, creating exciting possibilities for the future.

For instance, NFTs can add a new dimension to DeFi lending platforms. Currently, these platforms allow users to take loans against crypto assets. But what if you could do the same with NFTs? Imagine using your digital art collection or rare gaming items as collateral for a loan. This could unlock the financial value of NFTs, allowing owners to access liquidity without selling their treasured digital assets.

Next, we have the concept of fractionalized NFTs in the DeFi space. As discussed earlier, an NFT can represent a real-world asset, such as a property. By tokenizing and fractionalizing this property, multiple investors could own and trade their shares on a DeFi platform. This opens up a new world of possibilities for asset trading and investment.

And then there's the potential for yield farming with NFTs. Yield farming, a popular strategy in DeFi, involves users getting rewards for staking their cryptocurrencies in a DeFi protocol. With NFTs in the picture, users could earn rewards for staking their NFTs or even earn unique NFTs as rewards.

However, it's worth noting that the integration of NFTs into DeFi also brings new risks and challenges. For example, accurately assessing the value of NFTs for use as collateral in DeFi lending will be a complex task due to their unique and often subjective nature.

As the convergence of NFTs and DeFi continues to evolve, it's likely to lead to a more inclusive, efficient, and innovative financial ecosystem. We're just starting to scratch the surface, and the ensuing journey promises to be as thrilling as it is groundbreaking.

Future NFT Platforms

As we embark further into the future of NFTs, we see the emergence of new platforms and marketplaces, each offering unique features and services. The evolution of these platforms is shaping the trajectory of NFTs and the blockchain landscape.

For instance, consider OpenSea. Already a leading NFT marketplace, OpenSea continues to innovate by offering a wider range of NFTs, including art, music, domain names, virtual world items, and more. It has also recently introduced features like gas-free transactions, making it more accessible to users worldwide.

Another platform of note is Mintable, which provides a user-friendly interface for creating and selling NFTs. Mintable's mission is to simplify the process, making it easier for everyone, from artists to businesses, to mint and manage NFTs.

In the gaming world, platforms like Enjin are pushing the envelope. Enjin has launched an ecosystem that allows game developers to integrate blockchain technology and NFTs into their games, creating unique in-game items and characters. Enjin's innovative approach could potentially revolutionize the video gaming industry, blurring the lines between virtual and physical ownership.

Looking ahead, we can see projects in development that aim to solve some of the challenges that currently face the NFT space. Layer 2 solutions, like Immutable X, are being developed to provide scalability and environmentally friendly options for NFT transactions. This platform aims to provide a solution to Ethereum's scalability issues and high gas fees, which have been significant roadblocks in the broader adoption of NFTs.

Moreover, we're beginning to see the development of NFT platforms for specific sectors. For instance, Royal is an upcoming platform that aims to provide musicians a way to sell their music as NFTs and share their royalties with their fans. This platform, co-founded by electronic music producer 3LAU, signifies a new era of fan–artist relationships and could set a precedent for the music industry.

Each of these platforms represents a different facet of the NFT ecosystem, driving innovation and accessibility. As these platforms continue to evolve, they are paving the way for a future where NFTs are an integral part of our digital lives. Whether you're an artist, collector, gamer, or investor, keeping an eye on these emerging platforms can give you a front-row seat to the future of the NFT space.

NFTs and the Metaverse

A discussion of the future of NFTs won't be complete without exploring the potential of the metaverse. Think of the metaverse as a collective virtual shared space, created by the convergence of virtually enhanced physical reality and physically persistent virtual reality. In simpler terms, it's a world where physical and digital realities coexist and interact in real time.

Now, where do NFTs fit into this picture? NFTs, with their ability to establish digital ownership and uniqueness, are set to become a key element of the metaverse. Whether it's virtual real estate, in-game assets, digital identities, or even experiences, NFTs can provide the structure for ownership and trade in this digital universe.

Take, for instance, Decentraland, a virtual reality platform built on the Ethereum blockchain. Here, users can purchase land, represented as NFTs, and have full control over the virtual environment they own. They can create various experiences for visitors, like games or digital art exhibitions, or even rent or sell the land as they wish.

Somnium Space is another example of a blockchain-based metaverse where virtual reality intersects with NFTs. In this immersive world, every piece of content – from land parcels to buildings, avatars, and even sounds – is tokenized as an NFT, allowing users to own, create, buy, sell, and trade their assets in a shared virtual world.

Cryptovoxels is yet another virtual world where users can buy land and build upon it using a variety of voxel models. The land and items are represented as NFTs, and users have the freedom to explore, create, and trade in this digital sandbox.

The concept of the metaverse extends beyond just gaming and virtual worlds. Consider platforms like SuperWorld, which aim to build a metaverse overlaid on the real world. In SuperWorld, the entire surface of Earth is divided into 64 billion virtual plots of land, each represented as an NFT. Users can buy these plots and augment them with virtual objects and experiences, viewable through AR devices.

As the idea of the metaverse evolves, the role of NFTs within it is set to become increasingly significant. From creating digital economies to establishing digital identities, NFTs can provide the groundwork for this ambitious digital ecosystem. Looking ahead, as we become more interwoven with our digital lives, the metaverse will likely become a critical part of our existence, and NFTs will be the keys to this new kingdom.

What to Watch For

As we stride toward an NFT-infused future, there are several key trends and developments that should be on every digital enthusiast's radar.

1. Legislation and regulation: As the NFT market continues to expand, it will inevitably attract the attention of regulators. How will governments around the world regulate the sale and exchange of NFTs? Will they be treated as assets, securities, or something else? These legal definitions will have significant implications for traders and investors.

2. Environmental concerns: The environmental impact of NFTs, particularly those on the Ethereum network, is a point of contention. The process of minting NFTs and validating transactions requires a considerable amount of energy and contributes to carbon emissions. Keep an eye on developments around more eco-friendly blockchain technologies and the move to proof-of-stake consensus mechanisms, which could reduce the environmental impact significantly.

3. Interoperability: As more NFT platforms emerge, the issue of interoperability – the ability for NFTs to move and interact across different platforms and blockchains – will become increasingly important. Platforms that can ensure interoperability will likely lead the pack.

4. IP rights: How will intellectual property rights
    evolve in the face of NFTs? How will they protect
    artists, creators, and owners in the digital realm?
    The developments in this space could redefine the
    concept of digital ownership and have profound
    implications for artists and creators.

5. Digital identity: Look out for NFTs being used
    to represent digital identities. The idea of "self-
    sovereign identity," where individuals have sole
    ownership of their personal data and control over
    how it's used, could be facilitated by NFTs.

6. Cross-industry adoption: Keep a close eye on how
    different industries adopt NFTs. Which sectors
    will be quick to harness their potential, and which
    ones will face the most significant transformations?
    The music industry, real estate, gaming, and even
    healthcare could see radical changes.

7. Community engagement: Lastly, look out for NFT
    projects that place a heavy emphasis on community.
    As the world becomes more digital, NFTs that
    facilitate community building and engagement
    could become increasingly valuable.

As you journey through the captivating world of NFTs, remember that
the landscape is constantly changing and evolving. So, stay curious, stay
informed, and most importantly, stay excited for the endless possibilities
that lie ahead.

Summary

As we reach the end of our exploration into the world of NFTs, it is clear that we stand on the precipice of a new digital era. NFTs are not just a passing trend or a fleeting bubble; they represent a fundamental shift in how we conceive of ownership, value, and interaction in the digital world.

From the realms of art, music, and gaming to real estate, intellectual property, and even our own digital identities, the applications of NFTs are expansive and profound. Their ability to provide verifiable, non-duplicable proof of ownership in the digital realm is truly game-changing.

As we've delved into the future of NFTs, we've witnessed their potential to redefine industries, revolutionize financial systems, democratize access to assets, and even construct new virtual worlds. But it's worth noting that we're just at the dawn of this journey. The true potential of NFTs, especially as they intersect with developments in DeFi, the metaverse, and beyond, is yet to be fully realized.

Challenges do exist. Matters of regulation, environmental concerns, interoperability, and the protection of intellectual property rights are issues that must be addressed as the NFT landscape evolves. Yet, these challenges present opportunities for innovation and refinement.

In this ever-evolving digital age, the key is to remain adaptable and open to change. As NFTs continue to permeate various facets of our lives, we must be willing to learn, understand, and grow with this technology. Whether you're an artist, a collector, a gamer, an investor, or just an intrigued bystander, the world of NFTs holds something for you.

Glossary

Bitcoin

Bitcoin is a decentralized digital currency, without a central bank or single administrator, that can be sent from user to user on the peer-to-peer bitcoin network without the need for intermediaries.

Blockchain

A blockchain is a distributed database that is shared among the nodes of a computer network. As a database, a blockchain stores information electronically in digital format. Blockchains are best known for their crucial role in cryptocurrency systems, such as Bitcoin, for maintaining a secure and decentralized record of transactions. The innovation with a blockchain is that it guarantees the fidelity and security of a record of data and generates trust without the need for a trusted third party.

Cardano

Cardano is a public blockchain platform. It is open source and decentralized, with consensus achieved using proof of stake. It can facilitate peer-to-peer transactions with its internal cryptocurrency, Ada. Cardano was founded in 2015 by Ethereum co-founder Charles Hoskinson.

Cold Wallet (also Called Hardware Wallet)

A cold wallet is a physical device that keeps your crypto assets (e.g., cryptocurrency, NFTs) completely offline. Many such cold wallets look like USB drives. A cold wallet is much more secure than what is called hot wallet (see the following texts), since it keeps your crypto assets offline. The disadvantage is the possibility of losing your device and hence the assets that it contains. Cold wallet providers include Ledger Nano, Trezor, and CoolWallet.

Colored Coins

© Ahmed Bouzid, Paolo Narciso, and Steve Wood 2023
A. Bouzid et al., *NFTs for Business*, https://doi.org/10.1007/978-1-4842-9777-3

The term "Colored Coins" loosely describes a class of methods for representing and managing real-world assets on top of the Bitcoin blockchain.

CryptoKitties

CryptoKitties is a blockchain game on Ethereum developed by Canadian studio Dapper Labs that allows players to purchase, collect, breed, and sell virtual cats. It is one of the earliest attempts to deploy blockchain technology for recreation and leisure.

CryptoPunks

CryptoPunks are a set of 10,000 pixel-art images, with each being a uniquely generated character made by Larva Labs in 2017. Digital asset platform Anchorage helped Vis acquire CryptoPunk 7610.

Damien Hirst

Damien Steven Hirst is an English artist, entrepreneur, and art collector. He launched "The Currency" project, which involved selling 10,000 unique hand-painted dot-covered works on paper, each one corresponding to a non-fungible token. He is reportedly the United Kingdom's richest living artist, with his wealth estimated at $384 million in the 2020.

dApps

A decentralized application (DApp, dApp, Dapp, or dapp) is a computer application that runs on a decentralized computing system. dApps have been popularized by distributed ledger technologies (DLT) such as the Ethereum blockchain, where dApps are often referred to as smart contracts.

DAO

Decentralized autonomous organization (DAO) is a novel organizational structure that operates on blockchain technology, embodying a self-governing and automated framework. It enables participants to collectively make decisions, manage resources, and execute actions through transparent and programmable smart contracts. DAOs eliminate the need for traditional centralized governance models, instead relying on distributed consensus mechanisms and token-based voting systems to determine outcomes.

Enjin

Enjin is a blockchain-based gaming platform that focuses on making player-owned digital items like "NFTs" (non-fungible tokens). They offer ways to create tokens that can be used across multiple video games and can also be used across various platforms from PC to mobile. Enjin NFTs allow players to have true item ownership of their in-game items and trade them with others inside and outside of the game.

ERC-721

ERC-721 refers to a token standard that can be found on the Ethereum blockchain.

Ethereum 2.0

Ethereum 2.0 (ETH2) is an upgrade to the Ethereum network that aims to improve the network's security and scalability. This upgrade involves Ethereum shifting their current mining model to a staking model.

Everydays

A collage of 5,000 digital images created by Winkelmann for his Everydays series. Its associated non-fungible token (NFT) was sold for $69.3 million at Christie's in 2021, the most expensive NFT and among the most expensive works by a living artist.

Fidenza Line

Artist Tyler Hobbs' Fidenza Line consists of 999 unique Art Blocks depicting a pattern of colorful squares and rectangles which are generated via an algorithm. The series Fidenza #313 recently sold for 1,000 ETH, which amounted to just over $3.3 million USD at the time of transaction. The artwork was sold to the previous buyer for just 0.58 ETH (around $1,400 USD) on June 11, marking a truly mindboggling return within the span of two months.

Fractionalized NFTs

Fractionalized NFTs are NFTs split into smaller pieces by their original owner. They can be split into as little as two pieces or even billions!

This makes it possible for anyone to partially own iconic NFTs like CryptoPunks. When an NFT gets fractionalized, the pieces get locked into a smart contract.

FUD

FUD describes the spreading of "fear, uncertainty, and doubt" (typically through media). FOMO describes the "fear of missing out."

Gas Fees

NFT gas is the term given to the fee that most NFT trading platforms charge. This is incurred to conduct the transaction or execute a contract on their blockchain platform. Gas prices in Ethereum are denoted by unit of Gwei. It is determined by the amount of traffic on the network and the computation power taken to execute a transaction. To learn more about gas fees, please go here.

Hardware Wallet

See "**Cold Wallet**" earlier.

Hot Wallet (also Called Software Wallet)

A hot wallet refers to a virtual currency wallet that is accessible online, and it facilitates cryptocurrency transactions between the owner and end users. The most popular of hot wallets is MetaMask. Other hot wallets are WalletConnect, Coinbase, and Fortmatic (go here for a longer list of hot wallets). Note that because hot wallets are accessible online, they are more vulnerable to attacks than what are called "cold wallets" (also called, "hardware wallets").

Ledger

A public ledger derives its name from the age-old record-keeping system used to record information, such as agricultural commodity prices, news, and analysis. The public ledger was available for general public viewing as well as for verification. As cryptocurrency-based blockchain systems emerged, which rely on a similar record-keeping and public verification mechanism, the use of the public ledger gained popularity in the world of cryptocurrency. This article explores cryptocurrency public ledgers, how they work, and the challenges they face.

Mint

Minting an NFT is how your digital art becomes a part of the Ethereum blockchain – a public ledger that is unchangeable and tamper-proof. Similar to the way that metal coins are minted and added into circulation, NFTs are also tokens that get "minted" once they are created.

Mintable

Mintable is a Singapore-based, Mark Cuban-backed non-fungible token (NFT) platform. It is currently "striving to become the world's largest NFT marketplace by cataloging all NFTs ever minted on Ethereum as part of a major platform upgrade."

NFT

A non-fungible token (NFT) is a unique and noninterchangeable unit of data stored on a digital ledger (blockchain). NFTs can be associated with reproducible digital files such as photos, videos, and audio. NFTs use a digital ledger to provide a public certificate of authenticity or proof of ownership, but do not restrict the sharing or copying of the underlying digital files. The lack of interchangeability (fungibility) distinguishes NFTs from blockchain cryptocurrencies, such as Bitcoin.

NFTfi

NFTfi is a platform for P2P loans that use one of your NFTs as collateral for the transaction.

Nifty Gateway

Nifty Gateway is a digital art online auction platform for non-fungible token art founded by Duncan and Griffin Cock Foster and has since been acquired by the Winklevoss twins. Nifty Gateway has sold NFTs by Beeple, Grimes, LOGIK, and other widely followed NFT artists.

OpenSea

A peer-to-peer marketplace where goods such as gaming items, digital art, and other goods backed by a blockchain can be bought and sold.

Public Ledger

A public ledger derives its name from the age-old record-keeping system used to record information, such as agricultural commodity prices, news, and analysis. The public ledger was available for general public viewing as well as for verification. As cryptocurrency-based blockchain systems emerged, which rely on a similar record-keeping and public verification mechanism, the use of the public ledger gained popularity in the world of cryptocurrency. This article explores cryptocurrency public ledgers, how they work, and the challenges they face.

Smart Contracts

Smart contracts are simply programs stored on a blockchain that run when predetermined conditions are met. They typically are used to automate the execution of an agreement so that all participants can be immediately certain of the outcome, without any intermediary's involvement or time loss. They can also automate a workflow, triggering the next action when conditions are met.

Software Wallet

See "**Hot Wallet**" earlier.

SuperRare

SuperRare is an NFT marketplace to collect and trade unique, single-edition digital artworks.

The Sandbox

The Sandbox is a decentralized, community-driven gaming ecosystem where designers and artists can create, share, and monetize NFTs and gaming experiences on the blockchain and is partnered with many industry giants. Its popular virtual real estate, known as LANDs, are taking over the NFT world.

Wallet

Short for "crypto wallet." A crypto wallet is an interface that lets you interact with your blockchain assets. Crypto assets are essentially data on the blockchain. Crypto wallets contain the private key to their location on that blockchain, and this private key determines whether you can access that crypto. Crypto wallets are broadly classified as hot wallets and cold wallets. Hot wallets store the keys to your cryptocurrencies on an Internet-connected application, while cold wallets keep them offline, disconnected from the Internet.

Web3

This refers to a decentralized Internet paradigm that envisions a fundamental shift in online interactions and services. It builds upon the foundation of blockchain technology and distributed networks to enable a user-centric, trustless, and more open digital environment. Unlike the traditional Web 2.0, where data and control are concentrated in the hands of centralized entities, Web3 aims to empower individuals by allowing them to own their data, identities, and digital assets. It promotes peer-to-peer interactions, smart contracts, and decentralized applications (dApps), fostering greater transparency, security, and autonomy for users. At its core, Web3 seeks to reshape the Internet into a decentralized, user-driven ecosystem that reduces intermediaries, enhances privacy, and encourages collaboration through cryptographic protocols and decentralized technologies.

Index

GPSR Compliance
The European Union's (EU) General Product Safety Regulation (GPSR) is a set
of rules that requires consumer products to be safe and our obligations to
ensure this.

If you have any concerns about our products, you can contact us on

ProductSafety@springernature.com

In case Publisher is established outside the EU, the EU authorized
representative is:

Springer Nature Customer Service Center GmbH
Europaplatz 3
69115 Heidelberg, Germany